# Meditations on My Life as a Brooklyn Existentialist, Philosophical Paladin, and Samurai Thomist

Peter Anthony Achilles Redpath

En Route Books and Media, LLC
Saint Louis, MO

*Make the time*

En Route Books and Media, LLC
5705 Rhodes Avenue
St. Louis, MO 63109

Contact us at **contact@enroutebooksandmedia.com**

Cover Credit: Dr. Sebastian Mahfood, OP

© Copyright: Peter Anthony Achilles Redpath, Ph. D.

ISBN-13: 979-8-88870-248-2
Library of Congress Control Number: 2024948167

CEO, Aquinas School of Leadership, LLC
www.aquinasschoolofleadership.com

All rights reserved. No part of this book may be reproduced, stored in a retrieval system, or transmitted in any form, or by any means, electronic, mechanical, photocopying, or otherwise, without the prior written permission of the author.

# Table of Contents

Foreword by Robert A. Delfino and Marvin Peláez ................................... vii

Meditation Installment 1: Why I have decided to start writing a personal and philosophical autobiography ............................................. 1

Meditation Installment 2: How My Understanding of Philosophy/Science was Largely Formed During My Early Childhood and by age 5 had Started to get Me into Trouble .................................................. 3

Meditation Installment 3: How Brooklyn Existentialism Helped Fix in Me My Current Understanding of Philosophy/Science as Uncommon Common Sense ................................................................. 7

Meditation Installment 4: If Science is about What is Universally True, How can the Prudent Individual be the Measure of Scientific Truth in the Individual Situation? ............................................................ 13

Meditation Installment 5: How the Teachings of Socrates, Plato, and Aristotle about Prudence Turned Me into a Philosophical Paladin and Samurai Thomist ................................................................... 17

Meditation Installment 6, Part 1: My Definition of Myself as a 'Philosophical Paladin' and 'Samurai Thomist' Given in a Nutshell 21

Meditation Installment 6, Part 2: My Family Background ...................... 25

Meditation Installment 7: One Person's 'Organizational Crime Boss' is Another Person's 'Man of Uncommon Common Sense' ................ 31

Meditation Installment 8: Why Understanding the Nature of Qualities is Crucial to Living a Virtuous Life of any Perfection ........................ 37

Meditation Installment 9: How Human Beings Coordinate Use of Different Faculties to Observe and Understand Qualities and Their Behavior .......................................................................................... 41

Meditation Installment 10: Neighborhood Friends from Whom I Learned Necessary Principles for Becoming a Philosophical Paladin and Samurai Thomist .................................................................... 47

Meditation Installment 11: Reflections about Some Principles of Brooklyn Existentialism Neighborhood Friends Taught Me Essential to My Becoming a Philosophical Paladin and Samurai Thomist ...... 51

Meditation Installment 12: More Reflections about Principles of Brooklyn Existentialism and 2 Friends Who Helped Teach Me about Them ........................................................................................... 55

Meditation Installment 13: Fr. Robert Sirico as 'Brooklyn Existentialist,' 'Philosophical Paladin,' and 'Samurai Thomist' .................................. 61

Meditation Installment 14: 'Brooklyn Existentialism,' Michael Novak, Business as a Calling, Manichaeism, Greed, Duty, Honor, Conscience, and Public Shaming .......................................................... 67

Meditation Installment 15: How the 'Invisible Hand of Providence,' Senators JFK, RFK, Other 'Great Role Models,' and 'Camelot' Influenced Me to Become a 'Brooklyn Existentialist,' 'Philosophical Paladin,' and 'Samurai Thomist' .................................................. 73

Meditation Installment 16: How JFK and RFK had Enkindled in Me the Idea of Becoming a Professional Politician and Why, by the Late 1960s, I had Abandoned this Idea ........................................................ 79

Meditation Installment 17: 4 Evident First Principles, Truths, and Definitions a 'Brooklyn existentialist' Understands Early in Life about the Nature of Being a Leader, Leadership, an Organization, and Being an Organizational Leader .................................................. 83

Meditation Installment 18: Further Meditation on How a 'Brooklyn Existentialist' Conveys 'Communication of Mutual Understanding' (CMU) of Being a Leader' to Followers—and Especially to New Ones ............................................................................................................. 87

# Table of Contents

Meditation Installment 19: Gilson, the Decline of the West, and the Nature of Man as a 'Rational Animal'.................................................. 93

Meditation Installment 20: How Meditating about the Nature of 'Brooklyn Existentialism' Enabled Me Finally to Understand the Nature of Man as a 'Rational Animal' and How Such an Animal Behaves within the Individual Situation ............................................. 99

Meditation Installment 21: On the Nature of Man as a 'Prudent Animal,' the Integral, or Constituent, Parts of Prudence, and How the Virtue of Prudence Helps a Person Become a 'Master,' not a 'Victim,' of Circumstances ................................................................................ 107

Meditation Installment 22: Some Unconventional and Colorful Friends I had During My Youth Who Helped Me Start to Form My Understanding of 'Brooklyn Existentialism' as Essentially a Species of Situationally Prudent Behavior .......................................................... 111

Meditation Installment 23: How 'Augustinian-Sicilian, Political Prudence' is an Essential First Principle of the Colorful and Unconventional Behavior of 'Brooklyn Existentialist' Friends from My Youth ........................................................................................... 117

Meditation Installment 24: Paul Ranieri's and Vinny Palermo's Political 'Sicilian-Augustinianism' and Metaphysical and Moral 'Brooklyn Exis-tentialism'

Meditation Installment 25: 'Brooklyn Existentialists' as Political, Metaphysical, and Moral Enigmas ....................................................... 125

Meditation Installment 26: Why Understanding the Enigma of 'Brooklyn Existentialists' Like Carlo Gambino and My Friend Nick is Crucial for Personal Well Being Today ........................................................... 129

Meditation Installment 27: My Holy Saturday 2024 Lamentations with Dominic Profaci about the Contemporary Moral Decay of the United States and Dominic's Father's Unmatched Ability to Inculcate

Common Sense Through Communicating Mutual Understanding (CMU) .................................................................................................. 133

Meditation Installment 28: Brother Jerome 'Meric' Pessagno, CFX, and 'Tough Tony' Anastasia as Grand Masters of CMU Conversation ............................................................................................................. 137

Meditation Installment 29: In its Moral Principles, is 'Brooklyn Existentialism' a Species of 'Situation Ethics' and/or 'Moral Relativism'? ........................................................................................ 143

Meditation Installment 30: Recovering a Commonsense Understanding of Ethics/Moral Science and Metaphysics as Species of 'Prudent Situational Philosophizing' (PSP) ........................................................ 149

Meditation Installment 31: An Introductory Reflection about First Principles of Ethics and Morality 'Properly and not Properly Understood' ................................................................................................ 153

Meditation Installment 32: Voluntary, Freely Chosen, and Moral Activities 'Properly Understood' as 'Complicated Psychosomatic Practical Judgments' ............................................................................. 157

Meditation Installment 33: Why Accurately Judging Voluntary and Involuntary Moral Behavior is a Skill Crucial for Every Organizational Leader to Possess ................................................................. 161

Meditation Installment 34: Further Meditation about Why Every Investigation into First Principles Must Start Negatively and Some Astounding Implications of This Fact .......................................... 165

Meditation Installment 35: Some Astounding Implications that Intellectually Follow from the Fact that 'Unity is the Measure of All Things'—and their Crucial Importance for the Contemporary World ........................................................................................................... 169

Meditation Installment 36: Removing Some More Contemporary Misunderstandings regarding Aquinas's Teachings about the Nature of Philosophy/Science ....................................................................... 173

# Table of Contents

Meditation Installment 37: Additional Meditation about St. Thomas's Teachings Related to Philosophy, Science, Contrary Opposites, and Substance ........................................................................................ 177

Meditation Installment 38: Groundbreaking Meditation on St. Thomas Aquinas's Report of Aristotle's Depiction of the Origin of the World-Historical Concept of Philosophy, Science! ....................................... 183

Meditation Installment 39: Aquinas's Meditation about Philosophers, Like Ancient Poets, Being 'Myth-lovers' and 'Pursuers of Wisdom for Its Own Sake' ............................................................................. 187

Meditation Installment 40: Further Meditation on Aquinas's Teaching That Philosophy is Chiefly 'Pursuit of Wisdom for Its Own Sake' ........................................................................................................ 193

Meditation Installment 41: On How Aristotle and Aquinas Used Historical Study of the Nature of Causes Progressively to Explain Philosophy's Nature as 'Metaphysical Wonder' about Contrary Opposites ........................................................................................ 199

# —Foreword—

### *Samurai Thomism: A Solution to the Leadership Crisis*

Peter Anthony Achilles Redpath began his philosophical quest for truth as a young boy in Dyker Heights, Brooklyn, by asking what he believed were common sense questions and observing the dynamics of various organizations, including families, schools, churches, friendships, and businesses of all kinds. This early curiosity eventually led him to a vocation in philosophy, culminating in a long career as a philosophy professor at St. John's University in New York.

After a 40-year career in research and teaching, Redpath continued to refine and teach a philosophy rooted in the observations and questions of his youth. He realized that what he once considered common sense was actually "uncommon common sense," a trait he found increasingly absent in today's organizations —a sign of the current leadership crisis. Ultimately, Redpath believes this crisis stems from society's diminished understanding of the philosophical principles of sense realism, as embodied in Aristotle and especially by Saint Thomas Aquinas.

At the core of Redpath's Thomism is an emphasis on the human soul, its faculty psychology, and the relation different habits of the soul have to the perfection of human beings. Drawing on insights from Thomists such as Étienne Gilson, Jacques Maritain, Mortimer J. Adler, Armand Maurer, and Charles Bonaventure Crowley, among others, Redpath has appropriated and resuscitated aspects of

Aquinas's thought often ignored, obscured, or misunderstood in the history of Thomism.[1]

For example, from Maurer, Redpath developed Aquinas's distinction between the logical genus and the philosophical, or real genus.[2] Whereas a logical genus abstracts from all existence, a real or philosophical genus considers something as it exists in extra-mental reality and as it acts to generate something. For example, a healthy human body generates and sustains health for the person in question. With help from Crowley, Redpath further developed this notion of real genus, by resuscitating Aquinas's notion of virtual quantity.[3]

'Virtual quantity' in Latin is 'quantitas virtualis' and the adjective 'virtualis' comes from the Latin noun 'virtus,' meaning strength,

---

[1] For a brief discussion of some of these influences upon Redpath, see Peter A. Redpath, "The Nature of Common Sense and How We Can Use Common Sense to Renew the West" *Studia Gilsoniana* 3: supplement (2014): 455–484.

[2] For the distinction between the logical genus and the philosophical, or real genus, see Thomas Aquinas, *Summa theologiae,* I, q. 66, 2 ad 2 and *Summa theologiae* I, q. 88, 2, ad 4. With respect to Maurer, see Thomas Aquinas, *Expositio super Librum Boethii de Trinitate*, trans. Armand A. Maurer, *The Division and Methods of the Sciences* (Toronto: Pontifical Institute of Medieval Studies, 4th rev. ed., 1986), 83, note 15 and his "Introduction" vii-xli.

[3] Charles B Crowley, *Aristotelian-Thomistic Philosophy of Measure and the International System of Units (SI): Correlation of the International System of Units and the Philosophy of St. Thomas Aquinas and Aristotle*. Edited with a prescript by Peter A. Redpath (Lanham, Md.: University Press of America, 1996).

power, excellence, etc. As such, virtual quantity concerns the level of power and perfection of some nature or form. Concerning measurements or judgments about virtual quantity, Aquinas wrote the following:

> [V]irtual quantity is measured by the effects of the form. Now the first effect of form is being, for everything has being by reason of its form. The second effect is operation, for every agent acts through its form. Consequently virtual quantity is measured both in regard to being and in regard to action: in regard to being, forasmuch as things of a more perfect nature are of longer duration; and in regard to action, forasmuch as things of a more perfect nature are more powerful to act.[4]

Virtual quantity allows one to measure contraries within a real genus. Consider the contraries of a vibrantly healthy man vs. a very sick man. The very sick man still possesses a small degree of health to the extent that he is still alive. This notion of contrary is different from the notion of contrary in Aristotelian logic. In Aristotelian logic, contraries, such as "All Cats are Black" and "No Cats are Black" are mutually exclusive. If "No Cats are Black" is true then cats do not possess blackness at all. However, the sick and healthy

---

[4] Aquinas, *Summa theologiae*, I, q. 42, 1, ad 1, in *Summa theologiae: Prima Pars, 1-49*, ed. John Mortensen and Enrique Alarcón, trans. Laurence Shapcote (Lander, WY: Aquinas Institute for the Study of Sacred Doctrine, 2012), 426.

man both possess health to some degree, as measured by virtual quantity.

All these insights allow Redpath to conceive of the real genus as an organizational whole (a multiplicity of parts) that produces necessary properties (that is, *per se* accidents).[5] Additionally, Redpath argues that the study of how the real genus acts to produce these necessary properties is nothing other than science/philosophy. For example, the science of medicine studies the genus 'healthy body' and it is helpful to understand this real genus as an organization of parts (such as the heart and lungs) ordered to a goal (health). By understanding how these parts interact to cause health, and how, under some circumstances, they can also cause the contrary of health (disease), we can recognize when patients are ill and we can help treat them so that they will get well.

Pulling all of these insights together, we see that Redpath understands science/philosophy not as a body or system of knowledge, but as a habit of the soul directed to understanding real organizations (genera in the extra-mental world).[6] Arguing from this position, allows Redpath to do two important things. First, it allows him to argue that there is no *essential* difference between ancient Greek sense realist philosophy and modern experimental science. Despite some

---

[5] See Robert A. Delfino, "Redpath on the Nature of Philosophy" *Studia Gilsoniana*, vol. 5:1 (January–March 2016): 33-53.

[6] On this first point, see Armand A. Maurer, "The Unity of a Science: St. Thomas and the Nominalists," in *St. Thomas Aquinas, 1274-1974, Commemorative Studies*, vol. 2, ed. Armand A. Maurer (Toronto: Pontifical Institute of Mediaeval Studies, 1974), 269-291.

differences in method, they are united by their study of organizations and the necessary properties those organizations produce. This helps to end the centuries old schism between science and philosophy, which is no small feat.[7]

Second, Redpath's broader notion of science/philosophy allows there to be a science of ethics and a science of leadership, to give some examples. Redpath treats the contributions of his version of Thomism to ethics in his book *The Moral Psychology of St. Thomas Aquinas: An Introduction to Ragamuffin Ethics*. We will not cover those contributions here, because Arthur William McVey has already discussed them in his foreword to that book.[8] Instead, here, we wish to discuss Redpath's contribution to solving the leadership crisis in the modern world.

With respect to the topic of leadership, Redpath calls his philosophy *Samurai Thomism*. The term might seem unusual and anachronistic from a modern social science perspective. However, despite being in different times and cultures Aquinas and Miyamoto Musashi, the seventeenth-century Samurai and Ronin warrior, were both sense realists who came to very similar principles. In the case of Musashi, his principles were proven on the battlefield and in over fifty duels to the death. Additionally, both Musashi and Aquinas

---

[7] See Peter A. Redpath, *A Not-So-Elementary Christian Metaphysics: Written in the Hope of Ending the Centuries-Old Separation between Philosophy and Science and Science and Wisdom*, Vol. 1 (Manitou Springs, Co.: Socratic Press, 2012); reprinted by En Route Books and Media, 2015.

[8] Arthur William McVey, "Foreword," in Peter A. Redpath, *The Moral Psychology of St. Thomas Aquinas: An Introduction to Ragamuffin Ethics* (En Route Books & Media: St. Louis, Mo., 2017), 1-17.

were men of what Redpath calls "uncommon common sense" (a phrase Redpath borrowed from Mortimer Adler)—that is, men of prudence or practical wisdom. Finally, both wrote on science/philosophy.

Toward the end of his life, Musashi reflected deeply on his life experiences, the principles he honed, and he produced something close to a scientific account of the principles and causes of victory in combat in his famous *Book of Five Rings* (*Go Rin No Sho*).[9] The *Book of Five Rings*, a long-time staple on leadership reading lists, has already been studied by philosophically-minded leaders seeking wisdom in leadership.[10] However, Redpath not only analogously transposes some of Musashi's principles so they can be applied to the science of leadership, he also uses Aquinas's practical wisdom and metaphysics to justify, enhance, and occasionally correct them.[11]

But Redpath goes further. He explains why contemporary academic philosophy, whether Enlightenment or post-Enlightenment

---

[9] There are many translations of Musashi's *Book of Five Rings*; we recommend *The Book of Five Rings*, translated by William Scott Wilson (Boston and London: Shambhala, 2012).

[10] See, for example, Donald G. Krause, *The Book of Five Rings for Executives: Musashi's Classic Book of Competitive Tactics* (London: Nicholas Brealey Publishing Ltd, 2001).

[11] In *Summa theologiae*, II-II, q. 47, a. 13, Aquinas raises the question of "whether prudence can be in sinners?" In his reply he distinguishes among three kinds of prudence: false prudence, real but imperfect prudence, and perfect prudence. The third kind of prudence cannot exist in sinners, but the second kind can. Insofar as some of the figures Redpath discusses, such as Miyamoto Musashi and Tony Anastasio, embody real but imperfect prudence, they are subject to correction.

philosophy, makes it nearly impossible to solve the leadership crisis. Just as errors concerning the Trinity helped the Church to refine its teaching on the Trinity, the failures of contemporary world leaders and academics have helped Redpath to refine his Thomism.[12]

Consider the following. If science is a habit of the soul and a sense realism about real organizations (genera in the extra-mental world) that seeks to understand how its necessary properties are generated, then science is impossible without the human soul, its faculty psychology, its habits, and the ability of humans to grasp the real natures of things.[13] But these are precisely the things denied by most contemporary academics.

Indeed, popular materialist conceptions of human nature reject the soul and its faculty psychology. In addition, science is often conceived as a body or system of knowledge, not as a habit of the soul. Finally, the existence of a real natures is either held to be unknowable or is denied in favor of some kind of nominalism or social constructionism.

In his autobiography, Redpath avoids these errors and lays out in detail what is necessary for a good science of leadership. He argues that leadership is a communication skill that produces mutual understanding, which orders harmoniously a multitude of people (the

---

[12] Peter A. Redpath, "14 Evident Truths from the Organizational Genius of St. Thomas Aquinas: How 'Born Again Thomism' Can Help Save the West from Cultural Suicide" *Studia Gilsoniana*, 9, no. 4 (October–December 2020): 625–650.

[13] Peter A. Redpath, "The Essential Connection between Commonsense Philosophy and Leadership Excellence" *Studia Gilsoniana* 3: *supplement* (2014): 605–617.

team) so they can achieve a chief goal or *telos*. The leader must have a good understanding of human nature and of the level of talent/skill (virtual quantity) of the individual team members so he or she can bring out the best of the team by overcoming any resistance in the team and utilizing the team's receptivity to be led. Virtual quantity can also be used to assess a leader's effectiveness by measuring the leader's power to influence and inspire an organization of human persons to achieve a common goal.

As an example, consider the leader of a bunch of fire-fighters. A good leader must communicate mutual understanding to the team so that the multitude of people who comprise the team will act harmoniously to achieve the chief end, which, in this case, is putting out the fire. Here we see Redpath's notion of the real genus as a generator of necessary properties analogously applied to cover the fire-fighting team as a generator of extinguishing fires.

Concerning faculty psychology, for Redpath, a good leader is a behavioral psychologist with the virtue of prudence. As Aquinas says, "it belongs to prudence ... to apply right reason to action ... [and] to counsel, judge and command concerning the means of obtaining a due end."[14] Prudence enables a person to induce the means (the proper doable deed) to achieve the proper end in a particular situation, by making use of the cogitative internal sense, which Aquinas also calls particular reason. In non-human animals the cogitative sense is called the estimative sense, and it instinctually allows non-human animals (e.g., sheep) to induce something as dangerous

---

[14] Aquinas, *Summa theologiae*, II-II, q. 47, a. 4, reply and II-II, q. 47, a. 10, reply; trans. Shapcote, 448 and 455.

or useful. However, in humans, the cogitative sense also works with a collection of ideas stored in our memory and with our emotions of fear, hope, pleasure, and pain.

Consider, for example, a situation where a fire-fighting team is extinguishing fires in a three-story building. They used water to extinguish the fires on the first two floors. However, when they arrive on the third floor, the leader of the fire-fighting team hears the sparking of wires. This is a sound he has heard before and through his cogitative sense, he immediately induces *Danger—Electrical fire!* A few nanoseconds later, the intellectual virtue of prudence helps the leader to induce the <u>middle term</u> of a practical syllogism, which helps the leader infer the proper means to solve the problem at hand:

<u>Electrical fires</u> *cannot be put out by water.*
*This fire is an <u>electrical fire.</u>*
*This fire cannot be put out by water—use the special ABC extinguishers!*

Samurai Thomism is the culmination of Redpath's more than 50 years of philosophical reflection on contemporary leadership challenges, which seeks to reintegrate philosophical wisdom into all aspects of life. Samurai Thomism transcends time, space, and culture in the sense that two sense realists in different times and cultures came to very similar principles concerning how to achieve a chief end in the real world. Finally, Samurai Thomism is crucial because problems cannot be solved by wishing or hoping we can solve them; problems can only be solved by understanding the real natures of the things causing the problems and by using prudence to select the correct means to solve them.[15] This is the message Redpath has for the world—a message that deserves to be heard—especially considering the current leadership crisis facing the contemporary world.

Robert A. Delfino
Associate Professor
St. John's University, New York, United States

Marvin Peláez
PhD Candidate
The John Paul II Catholic University of Lublin, Poland

September 7, 2024

---

[15] In this context, Redpath is fond of quoting this passage from Gilson: "the history of philosophy is to the philosopher what his laboratory is to the scientist; it particularly shows how philosophers do not think as they wish, but as they can, for the interrelation of philosophical ideas is just as independent of us as are the laws of the physical world. A man is always free to choose his principles, but when he does he must face their consequences to the bitter end." Étienne Gilson, *The Unity of Philosophical Experience*, (San Francisco: Ignatius Press, 1999), 95.

# Meditation Installment 1

*Why I have decided to start writing a personal and philosophical autobiography*

Hello, as a participant in a revised and updated course on Samurai Thomism, or simply as a reader who has come across my work in some other way, to some extent, you know me and have some interest in understanding my philosophical work.

To assist you in so doing and to help my colleagues Sensei Marvin Pelaez and Dr. Robert Delfino market a revised and updated version of this class, with some reservation, I have decided I should start to write a philosophical and personal autobiography related to my 'unusual'—or (as Jude P. Dougherty has called it) my "unconventional" understanding of philosophy.

In designating my teachings in this way, Jude was referring to my repeated claim that, 'strictly speaking' and 'properly understood': (1) philosophy is identical with science; and (2) both philosophy and science are individual and trans-generational species of behavioral organizational psychology. 'Strictly speaking' and 'properly understood,' they are not 'bodies of knowledge' or species of 'systematic logic'—as they have been frequently misunderstood to be over the past several centuries and continue to be so misunderstood.

For mainly two reasons, I said above that I have set about writing this philosophical and personal autobiography 'with some reservation.'

One is because, for the past two years, I have been undergoing numerous medical treatments and operations for stomach and pancreatic cancer. How much of it I will eventually be able to complete, I do not know.

Right now, I am doing quite well physically and psychologically. So, starting to work on this autobiography now appears to me to be prudent.

A second reason is because writing a personal and philosophical autobiography for a general reading public might appear to some people to be arrogant, hubristic. Perhaps it is. I do not know; but I do not recall anyone ever accusing me of lacking in arrogance and hubris.

Hopefully, those who are taking this course or simply reading this autobiography will understand the chief reason I write it is simply as a pedagogical aid to help listeners and readers intellectually grasp how I came to arrive at my unusual way of viewing philosophy and science and their relationship to each other.

Peter Anthony Achilles Redpath

# Meditation Installment 2

*How My Understanding of Philosophy/Science was Largely Formed During My Early Childhood and by age 5 had Started to get Me into Trouble*

As I had explained in Installment 1 of this personal and philosophical autobiography, 'strictly speaking' and 'properly understood,' I understand philosophy and science to be: (1) essentially identical and (2) reducible to a species of 'behavioral organizational psychology.'

To date, no better, succinct exposition of how I arrived at this way of comprehending philosophy and science has been given than that presented by my colleague and friend Dr. Arthur William McVey in his 17-page "Foreword" to my book *The Moral Psychology of St. Thomas Aquinas: An Introduction to Ragamuffin Ethics* (En Route Books & Media: St. Louis, Mo., 2017).

Therein, from prior philosophical works I had written, McVey did a superb job making intelligible how I arrived at my conclusion that, more than anything else, philosophers/scientists are chiefly species of organizational psychologists—professional investigators interested in understanding how organizations can (1) harmoniously unify qualified parts to become born and grow to perfection and (2) die through corruption of these parts via internal disunity.

Centuries ago, in Book 1, Chapter 5 of his work *On the Heavens* (*de Caelo* in Latin), Aristotle had admonished readers that, down the road, small mistakes made at the beginning of an investigation (that is, small mistakes about essential first principles out of which investigations develop) eventually wind up "being multiplied a thousandfold."

Following Aristotle, St. Thomas Aquinas repeatedly had stated that: (1) science, or philosophy, is chiefly psychological habit (a habit of the human soul); (2) the whole of a science is contained in its principles; (3) the principles of a science are contained in its definitions; (4) and one of the principles contained in the definition of a science is that of science being a psychological habit of a scientist. In short, science, philosophy, only exists so long as scientists, philosophers, exist.

Related to me personally, philosophy/science started to develop shortly after my birth in the largely Italian/Irish, Dyker Heights, Bay Ridge, Brooklyn neighborhood in which I was surrounded on all sides by organizational geniuses possessed of uncommon common sense.

Related to people with uncommon common sense, several years ago, Bill McVey told me that philosophically I reminded him of Eric Hoffer. I agree with this comparison.

Reportedly, Hoffer once said, "My writing grows out of my life just as a branch out of a tree." Analogously, I say, "My philosophy/science grows out of me as a psychological disposition seeking perfect operation." Like all somewhat psychologically healthy beings, I was born to philosophize.

That this was so is evinced by some trouble into which, at age 5, my propensity toward philosophizing had gotten me into with a 'Cosa Nostra' family four houses from mine on 80th Street between 10th and 11th Avenues. For years I had fun playing with their daughter 'Babsy' until one day I had made the mistake of posing to her the metaphysical/moral problem that years later I would discover was known historically as the 'Epicurean Dilemma': "How can an all-good and all-powerful God allow so much evil to exist in the world?" From that day on I was no longer allowed to associate with Babsy.

# Meditation Installment 3

*How Brooklyn Existentialism Helped Fix in Me My Current Understanding of Philosophy/Science as Uncommon Common Sense*

Unlike I suspect most contemporary, professional philosophers and scientists, I did not come to my understanding of the psychological habits of philosophy and science in academia. A proper understanding of these psychological dispositions has been largely absent from there for centuries.

I came to it first on the streets of my Dyker Heights, Bay Ridge neighborhood. Over many following years, I added to this through different forms of practical and productive life and work experience in many different locations.

My friend and former colleague from St. Francis College on Montague Street in Brooklyn, Nino Langiulli (r.i.p) used to refer to himself philosophically as a "Brooklyn Existentialist." Decades ago, he penned a wonderful book he had entitled, *Brooklyn Existentialism*: *Voices from the Stoop Explaining How Philosophical Realism Can Bring About the Restoration of Intelligence, Character, and Taste* (Fidelity Press, 2008). I think that label fits my psychological disposition equally well.

In that book, Nino attempted to do pretty much the same thing many colleagues of ours and I have been trying to do for decades. He attempted to restore common sense in the form of moral, intellectual, practical, and productive prudence to the contemporary world.

The single best introduction to St. Thomas Aquinas's understanding of the nature of philosophy and science coming from his writings (not from a secondary source) is his discussion of the nature of prudence as he presents this in questions 47 through 56 of the second part of the second part of his magisterial *Summa theologiae* (2a2ae, qq. 47–56).

Therein, he states that all forms of prudence—observational as well as operational—are generated in the human soul through a psychologically innate (not acquired) habit (*habitus*, in Latin) to which in Latin he refers as *solertia*.

He adds that, to some extent, this quality is generated in all somewhat psychologically healthy human beings by possessing from birth some conflated disposition toward being 'shrewd' (*solers*) and 'quickwitted' (*citus*).

He asserts, further, that possessing these psychological dispositions causes a person—even an infant—to possess the quality of *synesis*: a psychological disposition that is the contrary opposite of a person in the state of *asynesis*. According to Aquinas, such a person is 'asinine'—lacks common sense (*Summa theologiae*, 2a2ae, q. 51, a. 3).

As St. Thomas sees it, practical and productive (concretely operational) prudence—and, subsequent to them, abstractly observational prudence—first develop within an individual and individual culture when, to some extent within that culture, the knowing activity of 'conscience' connects human activity to the natural law principle and prescription of 'Do good and avoid evil!' (referred to in Latin as the natural law principle of *synderesis*).

According to Thomas, conscience is simply the moral virtue of prudence—to whatever extent it has developed as a natural and acquired *habitus* (possession, having) existing within an individual or culture—to impel us human beings to do real good and avoid real evil.

In a way, conscience does this chiefly by psychologically sitting as a 'moral memory' in the form of a combined judge, jury, witness, prosecution, and dispenser of rewards and punishments essentially related to: (1) the excellence and beauty or ugliness and deformity of the soul of a human being and (2) some moral choice a person has made, is making, or might be considering to make.

For St. Thomas, prudence is the form of all virtue—moral, practical, productive, and intellectual. 'Strictly speaking,' he maintains that, without it, no human being, culture, or civilization can be habitually virtuous, talented, artistic, scientific, wise, or sane. Wherever and whenever it exists in any individual, culture, or civilization, the psychological habit of prudence is the chief, proximate cause of all philosophy/science.

Hence, 'strictly speaking': (1) an imprudently philosophical or scientific person can never be really philosophical or scientific; (2) an imprudently just person can never be really just; and (3) an imprudently courageous person is actually cowardly or rash—is not, and can never be, actually courageous at all.

An imprudent philosopher, or scientist, is asinine—a fool—the contrary opposite of someone wise. For the simple reason that he or she is a fool, is short on common sense, such a person can never habitually or non-habitually wonder about how to escape from ignorance so as to escape from the potential and actual damage ignorance can cause to an individual person being able to live a happy human life. He or she is not in touch with reality enough to do so.

Prudence is simply a species of uncommon common sense in the sense that, in whatever individual and culture it first comes to exist, it does so by prudentially reflecting on the behavior of people with practical and productive understanding (people with 'know-how' like farmers, sailors, businessmen, craftsmen) related to what causes different organizational wholes with which they are experientially familiar to behave the way they do.

St. Thomas tells us that, etymologically, the word 'prudence' is simply a contraction of the Latin term *providentia* ('providence'—being able to 'see ahead,' anticipate the implications of our actions). This is something fools can never do.

In addition, in what is often referred to as his famous 'Treatise on Law' *(Summa theologiae,* 1a2ae, qq. 90–97), Thomas maintains that the natural law is simply God's divine providence (prudence) as this applies to moral choices we human beings make.

By following prudence in our moral choices, we human beings do nothing other than measure our behavior to conform to God's prudence as contained within natural law as this applies generically, specifically, and individually to us living as rational animals—not as beasts!

When we intentionally behave in conformity with properly understood principles of natural law, we do more than follow brute, animal instinct. Through a healthy conscience, we conform our behavior to the rule of eternal, divine and human law as principles of human action that exist within the providential order: measures of divine prudence given to members of the human species by a providential God!

In its healthy form, conscience connects human beings to natural law, divine prudence, and sense reality. In so doing it: (1) stands as an obstacle to us becoming madmen and (2) essentially enables us to possess beautiful human souls through which we might achieve fully human perfection and live a beautiful human life in all respects in this life and the next.

Ignoring the voice of such a conscience is just plain damn dumb!

# Meditation Installment 4

*If Science is about What is Universally True, How can the Prudent Individual be the Measure of Scientific Truth in the Individual Situation?*

My simple response to the question I pose in Installment 4 is that, beyond being able to see the implications of our behavior in the future, by putting us in touch with sense reality, the virtue of prudence enables us to distinguish between: (1) two different meanings of 'possible' and 'impossible'; (2) two different meanings of 'truth' and 'doable deeds.

As Étienne Gilson had recognized in his beautiful, metaphysical, aesthetic book, *Painting and Reality* (New York, Pantheon Books, 1957), two species of possibility exist. One is abstract and conceptual. The other is concrete and really doable. Because they are out of touch with sense reality, imprudent people are unable to make this distinction.

Gilson states that abstract and conceptual possibility consists in being able intellectually to conceive of something the way logicians tend to conceive of it—as being abstractly non-contradictory according to a universal definition, no matter what the situation or circumstance might be. For example, for the logician, a human being is equally a human being with every other human being—no matter what the individual circumstance or situation.

Abstractly considered, all human beings are 'equally' human. Adolf Hitler and Mother Teresa are equally human. Neither is more or less perfectly human than the other.

Concretely considered, however, having common sense, the prudent individual recognizes (evidently 'sees,' 'induces') that Mother Teresa was much more human, qualitatively more perfect in being human, than was 'the *Fürher*'—who was more like a beast than a human being.

In the individual situation, the prudent individual immediately induces: (1) the causes that make an action doable in the individual situation, circumstance; (2) and the real means that can be used by this or that individual in this situation to effect a really doable deed.

According to St. Thomas, because he or she possesses the precise kind of prudence his or her job situation demands, the prudent individual, scientist, philosopher, sees the real means to a realizable end in the individual situation.

Through a qualitative 'Eureka! moment,' he or she is able to extract from a reasoning process some cause that connects the premises of a logical reasoning process to its conclusion—the middle term.

For this reason, 'strictly speaking,' the specific type of prudence (evident understanding/common sense) that a job demands is the essential quality that, more than anything else, causes someone to be an organizational leader in this or that discipline. Most of us, most of the time, have little-to-no common sense about most things. 'Common sense' is a simply a synonym for 'common understanding' of 'causes that get the job done' that are evidently known by practitioners of some applied knowledge.

Hence, for example, by sizing up the situation, the skilled pool player immediately induces just the right amount of 'English' to put on a ball to cause it to move into this or that pocket of a pool table. Analogously, a skilled golfer plays chiefly against the golf course (knows it like the back of his or her hand).

Any and every skilled artist knows the nature and qualities of his or her subject matter and the different ways it can resist or be receptive to taking his or her direction. For this reason, when they communicate with other professionals in their field of expertise, they tend to communicate by means of what logicians called an 'enthymeme'—a logical reasoning process that does not spell out every step involved in it. Instead, it assumes common sense, common understanding.

Because spelling out every step of an organizational reasoning process wastes valuable time and costs money or other resources, organizational leaders tend to assume understanding of the principles, causes, of an activity on the part of team members of the organization. They tend to consider team members who want every step of their reasoning process precisely spelled out to them to be annoying, and to lack organizational common sense.

I call such individuals 'encyclopedias open to the wrong page!' Organizational first principles of common sense are principles that need not be articulated to properly qualified team members.

They are not logical abstractions. They are concrete causes of action—essential means to an end—that that need to be executed in some individual situation, circumstance. No need exists to explain why they should be done in this or that situation. That they should be done here and now is organizationally evident—goes without the need to say why for anyone with organizational common sense.

According to Aquinas, the intellectual virtue of 'docility' or 'teachability' (*docilitas*, in Latin) is a necessary condition for becoming educated. St. Thomas maintained, further, that moral virtue prudence (which is a species of common sense!) causes docility.

He tells us that, before being taught outside the home, children generally learn some docility from their parents and their individual conscience—which should be shaped in a healthy way at home by their parents. In learning docility, he claims we all acquire some common sense (*Summa theologiae*, 1, q.13).

Since, 'strictly speaking,' common sense is the habit of rightly applying principles as measures of truth in immediate and mediated judgment, choice and reasoning, it is the measure of all right, sound, reasoning, no matter where this might exist. For this reason, the prudent individual is always the measure of all truth, including that of science, in the individual situation!

# Meditation Installment 5

*How the Teachings of Socrates, Plato, and Aristotle about Prudence Turned Me into a Philosophical Paladin and Samurai Thomist*

Well-known to anyone who has done extensive reading of Plato is that, in his discussion with the sophist Thrasymachos toward the end of Book 1 of his dialogue the *Republic*, he makes the startling claim that the power of injustice comes from the existence within it of justice as a species of prudence—a conflation of "wisdom and virtue" (351a).

In justifying this claim, Socrates maintains that, because injustice causes psychological disagreements and hatred among human beings no matter where it is found, no multitude of people that attempted to execute a common action (no human organization) could ever succeed in so doing if the members of this group were totally unjust toward each other. The love and justice that arises from their prudent treatment of each other as they go about treating other people hatefully and unjustly accounts for their short-term organizational success.

Beyond this, in his dialogue the *Phaedo* in which Socrates had recounted his early philosophical study of physics, or natural philosophy, he said he had to abandon this study because none of the teachers available to him at the time were able to make intelligible to him the common, or universal, cause for everything in the physical universe changing—coming into and going out of being (96a).

As he started to muddle along on his own way of wondering how to resolve this problem, he stated that one day he was pleased to hear someone reading from a book by the philosopher Anaxagoras that a mind which architectonically orders everything according to what is best for it (a providential mind) causes all change in the universe (97c).

Socrates added that, while he had had wonderful hope Anaxagoras could make intelligible to him how this universal mind caused order in the world, he soon discovered that this man never actually discussed this topic. He never got beyond the teachings of the ancient physicists that Socrates had found intellectually unsatisfying (98c).

This being the case, Socrates worked out his own theory that mind orders everything in the universe in relation to an idea of absolute beauty, or perfect good, that arranges all the parts of an organizational whole to be in perfect harmony to each other.

Based upon (1) what Plato had already said about justice, wisdom, and virtue in his *Republic* and (2) how, in the *Phaedo*, he had maintained that mind harmoniously unifies multitudes into parts of a whole in relation to some organizationally beautiful, or perfect, end, evident is that Socrates was thinking about this universal mind as a providential, or prudent, governor.

No wonder should exist, then, why centuries later, conceiving himself to be teaching in the tradition of Socrates' great student, Plato, and Plato's great student Aristotle, St. Thomas Aquinas would begin his masterful *Summa contra gentiles* by asserting that the "office," job responsibility, or duty (*officium*, in Latin) of the wise man is to "order" (that is, 'arrange') "things rightly and govern them well. Hence, among other things that men have conceived about the wise man, the Philosopher includes the notion that "it belongs to the wise man to order" (Anton C. Pegis, trans. Notre Dame and London, UK: Book 1, Chapter 1, n. 1; see Aristotle, *Metaphysics*, Bk. 1, Ch. 2, 982a18).

Nor should any surprise exist why, following in the tradition of Socrates, Plato, and Aristotle, Aquinas immediately continues:

Now, the rule of government and order for all things directed to an end must be taken from the end. For, since the end of each thing is its good, a thing is then best" (that is, beautifully or perfectly) "disposed when it is fittingly ordered to its end. And so we see among the arts that one functions as the governor and the ruler of another because it controls its end. Thus, the art of medicine rules and orders the art of the chemist because health, with which medicine is concerned, is the end of all the medications prepared by the art of the chemist. A similar situation obtains in the art of ship navigation in relation to shipbuilding, and in the military art with respect to the equestrian art and the equipment of war. The arts that rule other arts are called architectonic, as being the ruling arts. That is why the artisans devoted to these arts, who are called master artisans, appropriate to themselves the name of wise men. But, since these artisans are concerned, in each case, with the ends of particular things, they do not reach to the universal end of all things (*Summa contra gentiles*, Book 1, Chapter 1, n. 2).

According to St. Thomas, metaphysics ('first philosophy') and revealed theology are the sciences that extend to the highest and universal causes of everything. Since these causes exist in the mind of the author and mover of the universe (in an intellect), the ultimate end of the universe must be truth—the good of an intellect. Consequently, the focus of attention of a wise human being, especially that of a scientist, must aim at achieving truth (*Ibidem*).

In relation to particular sciences, Aquinas adds: "It belongs to one and the same science, however, both to pursue one of two contraries and to oppose the other. Medicine, for example, seeks to effect health and to eliminate illness. Hence, just as it belongs to the wise man to meditate especially on the truth belonging to the first principle, and to teach it to others, so it belongs to him to refute the opposing falsehood" (*Ibid.* n. 3)

Beyond this, according to St. Thomas, from what he has said above in his *Summa contra gentiles*, proper for someone wise is to: (1) "meditate and speak forth of the divine truth, which is truth in person" and (2) "refute the opposing error," including that of making false claims against religion—engaging in 'impiety.'

In short, in the spirit and tradition of Socrates, Plato, and Aquinas, today the office, duty, of someone wise is to become a 'Philosophical Paladin and Samurai Thomist.' Hence, no wonder should exist about why I decided to become one.

# Meditation Installment 6, Part 1

*My Definition of Myself as a 'Philosophical Paladin' and 'Samurai Thomist' Given in a Nutshell*

Because St. Thomas Aquinas had emphasized in his writings that: (1) being ignorant of the principles of a science at the start of an investigation eventually causes problems in that science afterwards; (2) the whole of a science is contained in its principles; and (3) the principles of a science are contained in its definition, prudence dictated for me to spend the previous 5 installments dividing into its real genus and species my precise definition of myself as a 'Philosophical Paladin and Samurai Thomist.' Having done so, in Part 1 of Installment 6 immediately below I can now provide that definition in a nutshell.

My real genus is that of a philosopher, scientist, and theologian considered as a trans-generational, organizational, behavioral psychologist. This is a social scientist who conceives of science, philosophy, and revealed theology, 'strictly speaking,' to be an individual and cultural psychological habit that is practiced historically.

By this I mean that I practice philosophy, science, and theology as part of a trans-generational, historical, enterprise or 'school'—the way the ancient Greek philosophers had first started to practice it going back at least as far as 'The Father of Western Philosophy,' Thales of Miletus (626/623-c. 548–545 B.C.). Philosophically and scientifically considered, this was the way Socrates, Plato, and Aristotle had done philosophy, science; and it was the common practice of medieval Catholic theologians like St. Thomas Aquinas.

Generically, I am a scientist, philosopher, and theologian who practices philosophy 'scholastically.' Etymologically the English word 'school' is derived from the Latin term *scola*— which means a place of leisure and learning. Practiced historically, philosophy, science, is part of a great trans-generational, respectful conversation in prudential, uncommon common sense.

Specifically, I practice philosophy, science, theology as a 'paladin'—someone who battles for an honorable cause—and as a 'samurai': a member of a professional class of noble fighters after the fashion of St. Thomas Aquinas. Habitually, I "meditate and speak forth of the divine truth, which is truth in person" and (2) "refute the opposing error," including that of making false claims against religion—engaging in 'impiety.'

Decades before I had come into contact with Plato's dialogues, I had learned from my parents and our neighbors in Dyker Heights, Bath Beach, and Bensonhurst how crucial for living a perfectly happy life is 'personal respect' for the commonsense power of justice and prudence. In a prior Installment, in fact, I had mentioned how not knowing how to speak prudently when talking to Babsy Donofrio about metaphysical and moral issues had one day gotten me into trouble with my parents, Babsy, and her parents.

Having such ignorance in my neighborhood at this time was very dangerous to a person's health, safety, and economic well-being. The neighborhood in which I was raised was not just a 'Mafia' neighborhood. It was the 'Mafia' neighborhood that controlled much of political, legal, economic, transportation, construction, waste disposal, media, educational, religious organizations and activity, and *cemetery burials* in the United States and internationally.

Joe Colombo, 'The Olive Oil King' Joseph Profaci, 'Tough Tony' Anastasia, and Vinny 'Ocean' Palermo lived within a mile radius of me. Colombo, Anastasia, and Palermo lived 3 to 4 blocks away from me—about 300 yards. Before I was out of elementary school, I knew much better than anyone in academia I have ever met who runs the United States of America and precisely how they run it.

In Installment 6, Part 2, I will start to explain how the prudential common sense of my father and his mother helped me flourish in these surroundings as a budding 'Philosophical Paladin' and 'Samurai Thomist.'

# Meditation Installment 6, Part 2

*My Family Background*

I was born in Brooklyn to Joseph E. and Alice B. Redpath on 16 August 1945 as the last of 5 children: Joseph (who died one day after birth); James (r.i.p., 10 years my elder), Robert (7 years my elder) and Kathleen (r.i.p.; about 3 years older than I was at birth).

My mother's father, who was Pennsylvania Dutch, Protestant, and from Kansas, had died of tuberculosis shortly after she was born. Her mother was Roman Catholic and, for some reason, had moved to the New York City area after her husband had died.

Because she had to work to support her daughter, she sent my mother to be raised by nuns in idyllic Kiamesha Lake, Sullivan County, upstate New York. As a result of her educational background, living with my mother was like living under the ever-watchful eye of a drill sergeant.

Sometime around 1933, the year she married my father, my mother wound up living in Bay Ridge, Brooklyn. After their marriage, she moved with her mother to live with my father in our home in Dyker Heights.

My father had been raised by his mother Katherine (aka, 'Kitty') with his two brothers (John and Bill) and several of his mother's relatives in Bensonhurst (during the fall, winter, and spring months) and in Breezy Point, Rockaway, Queens (during the summer).

Kitty Redpath was a big woman, at least 5' 7 inches tall. By the time she was in her 70s, she weighed over 300 pounds. She terrified me and many others!

Because he had been caught cheating on his wife, my father's mother had kicked his father out of the house. As a result, I never saw him, or even a photo of him. He lived in the Bronx and one of his jobs had involved working for the New York Yankees.

Aside from getting rent from several relatives who lived with her, my father's mother made her living by running one of the first trucking companies in New York State. One of my father's jobs as a youth involved working for her trucking company.

During 'Prohibition,' she became a bootlegger and ran a 'Speakeasy" and 'Floating Crap Game' out of her bungalow in Breezy Point. As a result, my father knew many of the saloon operators in Brooklyn and Queens; and when I went to visit her in Breezy Point, my grandmother always had a cold keg of beer on tap.

During his youth, my father used to work out on parallel bars in a local park. Somewhere I have a photo of him doing a handstand on the parallel bars.

The upper body strength he had developed from these activities combined with massively big and strong hands and his work on the delivery truck helped transform him into a star football athlete at New Utrecht High School—the educational institution made famous by John Travolta in television's 'Welcome Back, Kotter.' He was so good that he was offered an athletic scholarship to Columbia University.

Unhappily, because of his home situation, his mother told him he could not take the scholarship. Decades later, my sister told me he had reported to her that: (1) this was the first time he remembered ever crying; and (2) this made him resolve that, if he ever had children, he would make sure he would cover the cost of their college education.

Instead of going to Columbia, because of the close proximity of Breezy Point to Coney Island, my father opened a food stand across from Nathan's for the summer. (When I was a kid, he used to give me free tickets to go on the rides in Luna Park.) Also, he did manage to play at some time for a local, professional football team called the 'Brooklyn Giants'—before the 'New York Giants' came into existence.

Around 1929, my father and some of his friends joined the Archbishop John Hughes Council, Knights of Columbus (K of C) 481 in Dyker Heights and started to develop it. While permission to organize this Council had been granted in 1900, the Council on 86th Street and 13th Avenue did not have enough money actually to get started. Given its name, many of the members attracted to it in 1929 were Irish. Given its location, many were Italian.

To help baptize the new birth of the Council, with the help of some local Irish police, when he got married in 1933, my father had the liquor and beer for his wedding reception at the K of C delivered in a 'Paddy Wagon'!

By the 1950s and early 1960s, together with numerous Catholic organizations, my father's K of C started to grow by leaps and bounds and become incredibly influential within New York State and nationally. This was largely due to the work of my father and K of C member Joseph Profaci (aka, 'The Olive Oil King')—the two leading community organizers at the time.

Among the many influential people my father knew from this time on were:

Judge Ross Di Lorenzo; Judge Luigi Moreno; City Council President Tom Cuite (the City Council during his tenure was more politically powerful in NYC than that of the Mayor); Republican Lieutenant Governor under Nelson Rockefeller and later Governor of New York Malcolm Wilson; Democrat Governor of New York Hugh Carey; New York City Council Minority Leader, Republican Angelo Arculeo; Brooklyn Democrat Borough President Howard Golden; Republican New York State Senator and Assemblyman Chris Mega; Democrat New York City Councilman Sal Albanese; New York State Conservative Party Leader and New York City Conservative Party City Councilman Mike Long; New York City Police Commissioner Pat Murphy; New York City Board of Education President Bernie Donovan; Archbishop of New York Cardinal Terence Cooke

Politically, my father was an independent. On the national level, he tended to vote for Republicans because he said that, nationally and internationally, Democrats tend to get the U.S. involved in a war. On the local level, he tended to vote Democrat because he said they tended to fight harder than Republicans to bring in money to the local community.

During the time my father was Grand Knight of his K of C, he started to organize dozens of clubs, social events, and other activities for local parishes, schools, clubs, and so on. Every night after he got home from work, he would go out for several hours to do some charitable work—usually for more than one organization. As a result of his work, the Catholic Church in New York raised tremendous amounts of money.

On Friday and Saturday evenings, he would go to the K of C and usually return after midnight—at times as late as 1:00 AM.

My mother had a habit of checking out the different bedrooms in our house every evening about 11:30 PM. If we were not in our beds, she would pull back the cover from our pillow.

After we got in and had gotten to sleep, she would come into the room and slam open the window so that it would make noise and wake us up. Then she would start to yell at us for coming in late. In the winter, cold air would blow on our heads, which were right under the windows.

This did not bother my father because he had a deaf ear, and he used to sleep with it up so he could not hear my mother speaking. Plus, once he got to sleep, pretty much nothing could wake him up.

Every morning, my mother would leave to go Church to make 6:30 AM Mass. Before she left, if we had come in after her 11:30 PM curfew, she made sure to wake us up and start complaining about us coming in late.

She would keep this up relentlessly until we left the house. As a result, if we did not get in the house by curfew time, we would continually suffer from sleep deprivation; and we knew this would happen even before it occurred.

Again, this did not bother my father because, as she was going to Church, he would already be awake, and my mother would be driving him to the train station.

Just like his mother, my father was a man of uncommon common sense. In my next Installment, I will continue to meditate and report more precisely about what constitutes the psychological nature of this sort of unusual individual.

# Meditation Installment 7

*One Person's 'Organizational Crime Boss' is Another Person's 'Man of Uncommon Common Sense'*

While some initial and subsequent claims I make in these Installments might first strike some readers as downright false and even counterintuitive, I make them because decades of experience dealing with the subjects about which I write in these missives have taught me that what I am saying is evidently true to me.

At the same time, I can empathize with people who have an initial doubt triggered by some assertion I make because: (1) my first reaction to it when I first made it was likely the same as they have; and (2) even now I worry about whether a claim I make is accurate. For this reason, imitating a responsible social scientist and researcher, when I make a public assertion, I try to copy my claim to several colleagues I know to be rigorous scholars. I ask them to give me their professional reaction to what I have written.

One such claim I made in a prior Installment is that all human beings are born with a natural moral job, duty *(officium,* in Latin), to strive to live a life of perfect virtue—including moral virtue. In my last Installment, I provided a description of my family background and of some of our neighbors and friends—especially some of those of my father that many morally self-righteous individuals would claim could never have been naturally seeking to live a life of perfect virtue. Instead, they were criminals, and some were bosses of organized crime families.

One response I have to such individuals is, "The man who rings the bell at the brothel is seeking God." (The preceding quote is often attributed to the great English author and master of uncommon, common sense, Gilbert Keith Chesterton as its initial creator. However, it might actually have been first penned by a less well-known 20th-century Scottish writer in a 1945 work entitled, *The World, the Flesh, and Fr. Smith*). Whatever its initial source, the quote is a good one, filled with wisdom.

A second reply I have is that given by Saint Augustine in Book 4, Chapter 4 of his magisterial book, *City of God*: "Justice being taken away, then, what are kingdoms but great robberies? For what are robberies themselves but little kingdoms?" Put in a more contemporary way to fit contemporary American and international politics: "One person's 'organized crime boss' is another person's professional politician or contemporary three-letter governmental agency head."

As far as I can determine, as a result of original sin, no political government is democratic in the sense of being truly participatory and representative of those people that it has a moral duty to serve. At best, political governments (most human organizations) turn out to be benevolent despotisms or oligarchies.

The so-called 'organized crime bosses' and members of their organizations I came to know throughout my life in my largely Italian/Irish neighborhood tended to behave the way they did because the members of their respective communities tended to be treated like dirt—'disrespectfully'—by local political leaders, judges, businessmen, and other professionals. In a sense, in their behavior, these 'organized crime bosses' were simply following natural moral law prescription of self-defense as best their prior education had enabled them to understand it.

In the case of Joe Profaci, I find laughable a claim I often see cited that he created about 20 legitimate businesses and hundreds of jobs for employees. What an understatement! The man was 'a friggin' brilliant organizational psychologist and leader!

During his lifetime, directly or indirectly, he was personally responsible for creating dozens, perhaps hundreds, of business organizations and employing thousands of people in New York City and the United States in the food and beverage industries, restaurants, nightclubs, construction, and entertainment field—just to mention a few! Through his philanthropic work with the Catholic Church alone, he helped create dozens of businesses and thousands of jobs.

Italian businessmen like Joe Profaci employed hundreds of people I have known. Beyond this, they created dozens of youth organizations for young people to help them become educated to live virtuous lives.

I think that what I have said above becomes pretty clearly true if someone simply reads what St. Thomas states in his *Summa theologiae* (1a2ae, q. 1) to be the reason that to: (1) complete our education in prudence and moral virtue and (2) enable us to become as morally virtuous as possible, God had to provide human beings with a natural inclination to develop human law beyond the natural law—which all animals (including human beings), by a 'species instinct,' are inclined to follow as a behavioral guide in the individual situation.

In reply to the question whether God's naturally inclining human beings to develop a human law beyond natural law served any useful purpose, St. Thomas stated that, while all human beings have an innate aptitude and tendency to become virtuous and lead a life of perfect virtue, completely to do so requires education in virtue; and becoming perfectly educated in virtue requires discipline, hard work.

He added that no human being is naturally self-sufficient in becoming perfectly virtuous. We all need some help to become psychologically well adjusted to avoid pursuing unhealthy pleasures. Because of the shortness of experience they have had living their lives, young people have had little time to learn this educational lesson on their own. Hence, they especially need help from adults to do so.

Next, he observed that, by natural endowment or some early practical experience, all that young people require in order to make progress in making morally virtuous choices is a little periodic paternal warning in the form of encouragement to them.

Unhappily, however, St. Thomas had to admit that some young people are not inclined easily to be persuaded by words to stop being what today we might often call 'a royal pain in the ass.' Only habituation in doing virtuous deeds through fear and force: (1) restrains them from hurting good people and (2) causes them to leave them in peace. Aquinas called this schooling through legally enforceable punishment 'the education of law"—by which he meant the education in 'docility' ('teachability') that comes to a person through punishment by law.

In my next Installment, I will try to explain as best I can some other qualities we need to possess to lead the life of perfect virtue to which we are all naturally inclined.

# Meditation Installment 8

*Why Understanding the Nature of Qualities is Crucial to Living a Virtuous Life of any Perfection*

Before I can begin to talk about some additional, 'crucial,' qualities we need to possess to lead the life of perfect virtue to which all human beings are naturally inclined, readers should recall that I have already discussed one of them in some detail: prudence in the form of uncommon common sense. In addition, because St. Thomas Aquinas maintains that all virtues are qualities, before I can start to discuss other qualities, I need to explain what, first and foremost, Aquinas meant by the term 'quality.'

Doing so is especially crucial in our time because one of the single greatest psychological diseases with which modern and Enlightenment intellectuals have infected the West and the world over the past several centuries has been that qualities are not real. Instead, these charlatans claim that qualities are 'psychological fictions.'

If this false assertion were actually true, no virtue whatsoever could exist—including: (1) the moral virtues of prudence, courage, justice, and temperance; (2) the intellectual virtues of wisdom, science, and understanding; and (3) the liberal and 'fine' arts—aesthetic arts/arts of the beautiful! Time is long overdue for the contemporary world to toss this 'psychological crap' into the historical garbage bin where it belongs.

Far from being psychological fictions, as St. Thomas Aquinas rightly understood, 'strictly speaking,' first and foremost, qualities are causes essentially intrinsic to every real substance, acting nature, or organizational whole—the three of which he considered to be identical.

Aquinas referred to qualities by use of 2 technical, interchangeable, names: (1) 'intensive quantity' (*quantitatis intensiva*, in Latin) and (2) 'virtual quantity' (*quantitatis virtutis*, in Latin). Whichever term is used to name it, a quality as he understood it refers mainly to some *virtus* (intensity of causal power to move something, strength) existing within a subject; and it is simply a contraction of the term 'virtual quantity' (*Summa theologiae*, 1a-2ae, qq. 1 and 2).

Derived from the Latin term for man (*vir*), a comparable term we would use today for virtual, or intensive, quantity (or its contraction: 'virtue') would be 'manpower,' which we apply analogously to the term 'horsepower'—which is often used today to refer to the qualitative strength, greatness, size, or excellence of an automobile engine (St. Thomas Aquinas, *Commentary on the Metaphysics of Aristotle*, Book 5, Lesson 18, n. 1037).

Because virtue consists in qualitative greatness, excellence, by nature all virtue is essentially beautiful. For this reason, virtue is an irresistibly likable good. Because it shocks and arrests the attention of our sensory and intellectual faculties when we perceive the great magnitude and form of its perfection (that is, its beauty—the shocking good!), when we apprehend great acts of virtue, they incline us to jump for joy and applaud!

We do this not only in relation to experience of great moral virtue, like courageous acts. We instinctively do this when we witness a greatly performed athletic competition, musical performance, theatrical play, award winning movie, and so on.

Because qualities are essentially invisible to, and unobservable by, the external human senses, we can only experience, or measure, them in an externally sensory way by experiencing/measuring their effect on some physical body we can externally sense. For this reason, to experience, measure, a quality like weight (magnitude of heaviness), we have to try to pick up some physical object or observe what happens to a physician's scale when we step on it. Or we have to experience ourselves sweat on a hot summer's day or feel ourselves start to freeze on a cold winter's night.

We do not have to do anything so complicated when we want to experience, measure, the size of a piece of wood, the height of a tree, or how tall someone is. Hence, while determining the precise nature of qualities is somewhat complicated, denying their reality: (1) is absurd; and (2) absent divine intervention to save us from our own foolishness in doing so, condemns us to live a life of misery.

In my next Installment, I will write more about qualities, especially virtues, and how human beings coordinate use of different psychological faculties to observe and understand them.

# Meditation Installment 9

*How Human Beings Coordinate Use of Different Faculties to Observe and Understand Qualities and Their Behavior*

Just like the ancient Greek and Roman philosophers who had preceded them, Medieval Catholic theologians like St. Thomas Aquinas had considered the main job of someone wise to be to understand the nature and behavior of organizational wholes. A chief reason for this was because both groups: (1) had considered the physical universe around them to be a providentially guided organizational whole; and (2) were convinced that living a human life of any degree of happiness and perfection within such an organization essentially depended upon their understanding of how the essential and 'qualitatively unequal parts' of this whole harmonized to cause action.

Evident to them was that what we sometimes call 'Mother Nature' is both a great and a dangerous place within which to live. On the one hand, it provided the essential resources and nourishment to keep their bodies and souls alive. On the other hand, it was an environment filled with dangers and difficulties that could easily kill them.

As a result, their chief subject of interest as scientists was not logical abstractions, abstract mathematical theories, or poetic fictions. It was real, concrete causes qualitatively existing within, and influencing the behavior of, acting subjects: physical substances. These 'powerhouses' existing within real substances that caused them to move and act the way they do is what they chiefly considered to be their scientific, philosophical, 'first principles' and causes. Today, biologists display an analogous sort of interest in studying the behavior of cell mitochondria.

Since, by the time of Socrates, Plato, and Aristotle, they had recognized that real qualities (virtual quantities) existing within physical substances are the chief situational source, origin, of existing subjects (real substances) acting and being acted upon, real qualities became part of chief subject of study of later, major ancient Western philosophers. For this reason, they also became part of the chief subject of interest for Medieval Jewish, Islamic, and Catholic theologians.

According to St. Thomas, in his or her nature, a human being appears to be an 'organizational oxymoron': an animal with two qualitatively diverse souls harmoniously living one life together as an organizational unit. One soul: (1) is naturally immortal, naturally cannot die; and (2) naturally, qualitatively engages in moral (that is, prudent and free) behavior. The other soul: (1) is naturally mortal, naturally dies; and (2) naturally, qualitatively acts instinctively (that is, is in no way a moral agent—is naturally incapable of executing prudent and free action). Considered as such, numerically one human being appears to be essentially incapable of existing, much less of causing numerically one organizational action.

Undaunted by this paradox, St. Thomas explains that a complete, or perfect, organization has to possess and harmonize as many qualitative powers as complete organizational existence or life requires. In our case, by nature a human being has numerically one soul, not two souls.

This one soul has two qualitatively different parts, one (the intellectual part) is qualitatively higher and more powerful. The other (the animal part) is qualitatively lower and weaker.

Aquinas maintains that the intellectual part of the human soul possesses a faculty of understanding that abstracts from individual time, place, and situation. In and of itself, it can never execute a human act. In contrast, the animal part of the human soul possesses a faculty of understanding that St. Thomas says is analogous to, but not identical with, 'animal instinct.' In and of itself, it, too, can never cause human action.

Unhappily St. Thomas refers to this faculty interchangeably as 'particular reason' and 'cogitative reason.' I call referring to these terms the way he does 'infelicitous' because, both on the intellectual and sense levels, he is not talking about a faculty of reasoning. He is talking about 'an act of immediate understanding, induction, insight.'

Analogously considered, because they do not engage in abstract reasoning at all, when confronted by immediate danger, or some healthy good, brute animals cannot engage in a lengthy, abstract, logical, reasoning process in the individual situation. Instead, in the individual situation, by means of a faculty St. Thomas calls an 'estimative power' (*vis aestimativa*, in Latin) by which they are able immediately to sense safety, danger, utility, and non-utility, brute animals immediately 'jump to a conclusion' about an action they should execute.

St. Thomas states that when a lamb sees a wolf approach, because it immediately senses the wolf to be a natural enemy of lambs, the lamb immediately flees. It does not take time out to start engaging in composing a syllogism. Analogously, Aquinas states that a bird does not collect straw because it finds doing so pleasing to its senses. It does so because it needs the straw to build a nest. He even says that medical doctors during his time had assigned a location for the organ of this faculty in the middle part of the head! (*Summa theologiae*, 1a, q. 78, a. 4).

As the preceding examples indicate, in all animals, whether human or brute, what Aquinas calls the 'irascible' emotions, or passions, of hope and fear serve as commonsense principles of understanding by helping to keep each in touch with sense reality. In so doing, they help us to harmonize all human action into numerically one organizational operation of human and animal understanding.

This is the same sort of understanding about which, decades ago, the great uncommon commonsense Christian philosopher and theologian C.S. [Clive Staples] Lewis had sagely admonished us:

It still remains true that no justification of virtue will enable a man to be virtuous. Without the aid of trained emotions, the intellect is powerless against the animal organism. I had sooner play cards against a man who was quite skeptical about ethics, but bred to believe that 'a gentleman does not cheat,' than against the irresponsible, moral philosopher who had been brought up among sharpers. In battles it is not syllogisms that will keep the reluctant nerves and muscles to their post in the third hour of the bombardment.

The crudest sentimentalism . . . about a flag or a country or a regiment will be a more use. We were told it all long ago by Plato. As the king governs by his executive, so Reason in man must rule the mere appetites by means of the 'spirited element.' The head rules the belly through the chest—the seat, as Alanus tells us, of Magnanimity, of emotions organized by trained habit into stable sentiments. The Chest-Magnanimity-Sentiment—these are the indispensable liaison officers between cerebral man and visceral man. It may even be said that it is by this middle element that man is man: for by his intellect he is mere spirit and by his appetite mere animal. . . .. A persevering devotion to truth, a nice sense of intellectual honour, cannot be long maintained without the aid of sentiment . . . .. It is not excess of thought, but defect of fertile and generous emotion, that marks them out. Their heads are no bigger than the ordinary: it is the atrophy of the chest beneath that makes them so.

We make men without chests and expect of them virtue and enterprise. We laugh at honour and are shocked to find traitors in our midst. We castrate and bid the geldings to be fruitful (*The Abolition of Man* [New York: Touchstone, 1966, pp. 35–36).

In my next Installment, I will talk about people from my neighborhood who were rich in this middle element and helped me acquire some of it.

# Meditation Installment 10

*Neighborhood Friends from Whom I Learned Necessary Principles for Becoming a Philosophical Paladin and Samurai Thomist*

A major point I stressed in my last Installment was that every action we perform as human beings we exercise as physical and psychological, intellectual and emotional, organizational wholes. Whether we are explicitly conscious of this or not, whenever we see, hear, dance, sing, swim, play a musical instrument, or even read a book, we do so as physical and psychological, intellectual and emotional, organizational wholes.

Our feet do not dance without the rest of our body dancing. Our eyes do not see, nor do our ears hear, without us as individual, organizational wholes, seeing and hearing. Individual *persons* see and hear as psychosomatic, intellectual and passionate, organizationally whole units. The individual person performs and exists in all these acts just as the spirit of a team exists in all its team members.

The faculties of sight and hearing and the emotions of fear, anger, and joy exist within the human intellect. Simultaneously, the human intellect exists within all these faculties as they are being executed. As the great French historian of philosophy, Étienne Gilson, one said somewhere: "We sense with our intellect, and we intellectualize with our senses."

This is an evident, commonsense first principle of understanding for a 'Philosophical Paladin' and 'Samurai Thomist.' I first learned it at home and from 'great-souled,' childhood friends and adult neighbors rich in honor and commonsense passion centered around the missionary 'Shrine Church of St. Bernadette' (generally simply called 'St. Bernadette's'), located on 82nd St. and 13th Ave. in Brooklyn, a few blocks from my home.

The Church was founded in 1935 by Fr. Francis P. Barilla (friend of my father and, later, Monsignor). While it was being built, Fr. Barilla served Sunday Masses in the auditorium of the Archbishop John Hughes Council Knights of Columbus on 86th St., and 13th Ave.. The Church's location put it between the K of C and the Andrew Torregrossa Funeral Home (located at 79th St., and 13th Ave.). This placed the Church more or less in the heart of what, by the late 1950s, would be publicized in news media as the home of 'organized crime' in Brooklyn.

St. Bernadette's was the Church where Joe Colombo's 1971 funeral Mass was conducted. And, even though I have seen reports that he never had a funeral service in Dyker Heights, I vividly recall that one had been held for Albert Anastasia in 1957 at the Torregrossa Funeral Home. I clearly remember this because I was riding my bicycle to St. Bernadette's on the day of the wake. Even before I had gotten to 80th St. and 13th Ave., because I was riding downhill, I could see the Avenue was mobbed with people. It was the biggest crowd I had ever seen—so big I could not even get onto 13th Avenue!

Before the late 1950s, I had never heard the term 'organized crime' used, and I never would have associated it with my neighborhood. In a previous Installment, I had mentioned that St. Bernadette's and my father's K of C had established numerous programs that had benefited local young people.

# Meditation Installment 10

I know this to be true because I was one of these kids. I played baseball on one of the teams in St. Bernadette's baseball league. The Torregrossa Funeral Home helped fund this program. Joe Torregrossa was my first baseball coach, and one of the kindest, gentlest, men I have ever met.

Two kids with whom I became friends in this League were Jimmy Colombo and Joe Indelicato. Joe was my same age. Jimmy was a few years older than I was.

Jimmy used to walk with me to games. He would also play and watch out for me in the schoolyard of P.S. 201 on 80th St., between 10th and 11th Aves. whenever he saw me there. He also helped me learn how to fight against bullies. I still recall his kind, gentle demeanor.

Apart from playing ball on the same team with Joe Indelicato, I had not seen or heard from Joe for decades until one day, several years ago, he phoned me out of the blue to tell me that he had been given my name by Brother Owen Sadlier from St. Francis College in Brooklyn. He told me Brother Owen had suggested he contact me after Joe had told Owen he wanted to get the name of someone to become a member of the Board for an organization called the 'Catholic Education Foundation' Joe was starting.

In my next Installment, I will talk more about my neighborhood friends who helped teach me how to become a Philosophical Paladin and Samurai Thomist.

# Meditation Installment 11

*Reflections about Some Principles of Brooklyn Existentialism Neighborhood Friends Taught Me Essential to My Becoming a Philosophical Paladin and Samurai Thomist*

Being a philosopher as a 'Philosophical Paladin and Samurai Thomist' is an activity I consider to be a natural vocation of all physically and psychologically, relatively healthy human beings. Because it does not permit such a person to separate his or her personal life from his or her professional life, considered as such, it is simultaneously a blessing, exhausting, and often (as Socrates discovered) dangerous.

Unlike most other professional business people, as soon as I wake up in the morning, I start practicing my profession. In some way, all the dreams I have at night tend to relate to it. As a result, being a philosopher is physically and psychologically fatiguing.

At the same time, unless I go totally insane or become completely incapacitated physically, I can do it at all waking moments, anywhere and everywhere, without having to worry about supply and shipping problems or product spoilage. Who could ask for a more wonderful business in which to be involved on a lifelong basis?

I mention these facts at the beginning of this Installment 11 because, in Installment 10, I had said that doing philosophy the way the leading ancient Greek philosophers and St. Thomas Aquinas had practiced it essentially involves attempting to understand the nature and causes of organizational action. As they understood it, philosophy is organizational psychology, and philosophers are organizational psychologists.

Considered as organizational psychologists, we are also social scientists. We philosophize within the context of social groups that are political societies. Philosophy arose among the Ancient Greeks and was practiced by Medieval Christian theologians within schools as part of an intellectual tradition of prudential learning in the form of uncommon common sense intentionally transmitted from one generation to the next.

Within each of the Installments I write, I include what I consider to be evident principles/truths of philosophical understanding. I do this because, in spite of widespread misunderstandings to the contrary, philosophy, science, does not start with reasoning. It starts with understanding. To reason rightly a person must first understand what he or she is reasoning, talking, about. Not to proceed in this way is to be 'an encyclopedia open to the wrong page.'

Philosophically, scientifically, we must first precisely define our subject before we can start to reason well or badly about it. Scientifically, philosophically, we have to know precisely what we are talking about and how we are talking about it. These are evident truths.

Reasoning is a defective way of knowing. Far better than reasoning is to proceed immediately from understanding to understanding—the way St. Thomas Aquinas understood angelic intellects to operate.

As I learned from neighborhood friends in my youth, not to develop this psychological habit is dangerous, lacking in prudential common sense. Such foolishness is glaringly driven home in the comic strip 'Hagar the Horrible' in which Hagar had been assigned to be the nightwatchman looking out for approaching enemies from the top of a castle overlooking a moat. As he was doing so, a voice called out to him from within the castle asking him, "Is there any sign of an enemy approaching?" After Hagar replies, "What is an enemy?", a voice from within the castle responds: "Never make a philosopher a nightwatchman!"

While this might be true if a person mistakenly identifies a philosopher with a logician, this claim is not true of individuals who philosophize in the tradition of Aristotle and St. Thomas Aquinas. This is the tradition of Brooklyn Existentialism I learned early in life in Dyker Heights.

While 'professional politicians' might refer to some of my friends and neighbors in Dyker Heights as 'organized crime, bosses,' decades of experience at living have convinced me that most professional politicians are 'organized crime bosses.' If I were to identify one person from my neighborhood that definitely deserves that title, in my opinion, it would be Anthony Fauci.

For most of my life, I have known that professional politicians tend to be organized crime bosses. Unhappily, some people I have known for decades are just beginning to discover this fact. As a result, they have lost their cultural bearings and are becoming increasingly depressed. One reason I am writing these Installments is to help such people better understand their situation so that they can be better able to cope with it and even flourish within it..

In writing these Installments, I will often make reference to friends who were less than saints. In fact, some of them were sociopaths. I do not do so because I sanction criminal behavior or think lightly about it. I do so for at least two reasons: (1) I am somewhat of a cynic and adhere to Ambrose Beirce's definition of a 'saint' as, 'A dead sinner revised and edited'; and (2) very often people someone thought was a decent human being turns out to have been a wife beater and a child abuser.

Socrates realized the same thing about Zeus. As Plato's dialogue the *Euthyphro* indicates, one reason Socrates could not accept the depiction of the nature of a god given by the leading Ancient Greek poets was because the greatest of the gods, Zeus, was portrayed as being a cannibal who had eaten one of his sons, crippled another, and had beaten his wife.

The fact that some talented people might also be sociopaths does not mean we cannot learn anything from them. Sometimes sociopaths have a way of observing or doing good things that are true, even brilliant, which decent people cannot see or do.

In Installment 12, I will talk about two people I knew as a youth who were less than saints, but not sociopaths, who introduced me to principles of Brooklyn Existentialism that helped transform me into a Philosophical Paladin' and 'Samurai Thomist'—my friends Paul Ranieri (r.i.p; aka 'Paulie Walnuts') and Vinny Palermo (aka 'Vinny Ocean').

# Meditation Installment 12

*More Reflections about Principles of Brooklyn Existentialism and 2 Friends Who Helped Teach Me about Them*

In prior Installments I have emphasized that, as a 'Brooklyn Existentialist,' 'Philosophical Paladin,' and 'Samurai Thomist,' I do not think of philosophy as a species of logic that has as its chief subject of interest a logical system or body of knowledge. I think of philosophy in a much more complicated way—as an individual and cultural trans-generational, behavioral and organizational psychology; and I consider its chief subject of interest to be understanding the action, or behavior, of individuals within organizations that exist within individual situations.

Also, in prior Installments, I have indicated that, in each of these missives, I will reflect, or meditate, on the nature and causes of individual and organizational action. For this reason, right now I will start to talk about some essential principles involved in personal action that occur within organizations as these actions relate to choices human beings and organizations make.

The first is an 'insight' I got many years ago while reading the last chapter of Étienne Gilson's masterful *Unity of Philosophical Experience* in which he observes that 'philosophers do not think the way they wish.' They 'think the way they can.' Extending that principle to all human beings and to human choice, I immediately recalled Aristotle's and St. Thomas's well-known assertion about human choice—that, while we can wish for the impossible, we cannot choose it. Because we can only choose the actual, and since the actual is really possible, we cannot choose the impossible.

Meditating on that evident truth against the background of statements Socrates had made in Plato's dialogues immediately caused me to have a 'Eureka! moment' similar to that once had by Archimedes. Suddenly I realized that *the only object human beings can actually choose is an action or something related to an action.*

In those dialogues Socrates was telling his listeners that we never choose things; and the reason we do not do so is because 'we cannot do so.' For example, we never choose an automobile, a house, shoes, clothes, a husband or wife. We choose to: (1) 'buy or sell' an automobile; (2) 'purchase, sell, rent, lease, or own a house'; (3) 'wear shoes or clothes'; and (4) 'marry or divorce a husband or wife.' Furthermore, when we make such choices, we do so as human beings of real, limited abilities, existing within individual, 'human circumstances, or situations.'

The implications of the combined brilliant observations of Socrates, Plato, Aristotle, St. Thomas, and Gilson as they relate to human happiness are enormous. Beyond a shadow of a doubt, they indicate that, for the simple reason that we can never directly possess things, 'having things' can never make us happy!

Why not? Because we can only: (1) have actions and relations to things, (2) in individual situations, (3) to the limited extent our physical and psychological powers permit. Human happiness is caused by prudentially chosen and executed, situationally doable deeds.

At this point in my life, I realize I had not first learned these evident truths from reading Socrates, Aristotle, St. Thomas Aquinas, and Gilson. I had first learned them from my parents, siblings, and neighbors in Dyker Heights, Bensonhurst, Bath Beach, and Bay Ridge, Brooklyn, including from friends like Paul Ranieri (r.i.p; aka 'Paulie Walnuts') and Vinny Palermo (aka 'Vinny Ocean'). I had first learned them from people who had helped pass on to me the ancient wisdom of these great teachers from our shared cultural institutions and traditions.

I first met Paul when he was enrolled as a student in my fourth or fifth grade class at St. Ephrem's Elementary School. Like St. Bernadette's, St. Ephrem's was started as a Mission Church at about the same time St. Bernadette's was established. Even though my father had been very active for years at St. Bernadette's, at the same time, the location of our house put us within St. Ephrem's as our Church parish and elementary school. For this reason, my father became as equally active at St. Ephrem's, and in its activities, as he had been at St. Bernadette's and the activities of the K of C; and my mother joined him in many of these activities, and became involved in some of her own.

Because my friend Paul was not especially fond of studying, even though he was very smart, he had been 'left back' a grade at St. Ephrem's. This worried me because Paul had the reputation of being the toughest kid in the class a year ahead of me.

Before he had shown up, I had had the reputation—for which I had much prided myself—of being the toughest kid in the class. This was especially important to me to preserve because my brothers Jimmy and Bobby had had that reputation in their classes—and for being the toughest kids in the School when they had graduated.

When he had graduated at age 13, Jimmy had Paul Newman good looks, was 6 feet tall, weighed about 180 pounds, looked about 20 years old, was a great athlete, had a red-hot temper, and was a terrific fighter. My brother Bobby was about seven years older than I was. Like Jimmy, he was also a great athlete (he could have played professional baseball, but became a U.S. Marine instead). He also had a hot temper and was a terrific fighter—an especially good boxer. As Dominic Profaci once told me, "Boy, were they tough!"

Beyond this reputation, Paul just looked tough. He had jet-black hair with a short widow's-peak in it, piercing eyes, and he was all muscle. As one of my friends once said to me after meeting Paul when we were all teenagers, "That guy looks like he could eat your heart out!"

Not only did he look tough physically, the way he talked, walked, dressed, and behaved, made him look tough. He used to wear a 'Wolf-ring'—a ring with the head of a wolf on it. He always wore black, pointed shoes to school; and usually motorcycle boots in the afternoon after school—at which time he also wore a black motorcycle jacket with its collar always up during the fall and winter months. When he did so, he carried a switchblade knife with him. Even though he was not very tall (was maybe about 5' 8" as an adult), he stood and walked in a military fashion—totally erect; and when he walked, he did so quickly, slightly pigeon-toed, and with utmost confidence.

Because our seats in class were alphabetically arranged with 2 desks per row (about 60 seats in the class in total), Paul sat directly in front of me, and next to a mathematical-science geek named

## Meditation Installment 12

Thomas Paul Edward Quinn. For several reasons, Paul could not stand Quinn.

One reason for this was that Quinn was an arrogant jerk. A second reason was because Quinn used to pick his nose and put the snot on his desk next to Paul. One day after he had done this, I heard a loud 'Whack!' as Paul shouted "That's disgusting," and Quinn's body went bouncing on the floor with a 'thud.' Paul had punched him out of his seat.

I think I first met Vinny at the P.S. 201 schoolyard when I was with Paul. Vinny would come to the schoolyard a few days a week for a little bit of time. Paul and he used to play softball with me and other friends of ours.

I recall Vinny always eating a meatball hero sandwich he had brought with him, and drinking a pint of milk with it. Because he had to take care of a chronically sick mother at home in bed, Vinny could never stay very long playing. I think at the time I met him he might still have been an altar boy.

Like Paul, Vinny was all muscle. Like Paul, he just looked, talked, and walked like someone any person with real common sense would know was tough. I remember both of them, for some strange reason, deciding to tear out from the schoolyard a cement water fountain that had been installed maybe a week before.

This was no simple pedestal water fountain. It was about 3 feet wide and 4 feet tall. Nevertheless, they pushed and pulled it until it finally came out. Needless to say, many of us were not happy with them for having done this, and we complained to them about it.

I will talk more about Paul and Vinny in future Installments. For now, I will simply say that both of them drove home to me the crucial importance of understanding precisely the situation in which I existed, and how to flourish within it. In addition, more than once both had saved me from a well-deserved beating!

# Meditation Installment 13

***Fr. Robert Sirico as 'Brooklyn Existentialist,' 'Philosophical Paladin,' and 'Samurai Thomist'***

For this Installment, I have decided to focus attention on another friend of mine from the Dyker Heights area in Brooklyn: Fr. Robert Sirico. While I never recall meeting Fr. Sirico when I was a youth, I had met several relatives of his many times while dining at their famous Italian restaurant located at 8023 13th Avenue. This was the most-frequented Italian restaurant in our area, and aside from Denino's in Staten Island, it served the most delicious pizza I have ever tasted!

The first time I remember being in contact with Fr. Sirico was in 1990, when he had phoned to tell me he was planning to set up his famous 'Acton Institute for the Study of Religion and Liberty.' He asked me to give him contact information to help him do so. Recognizing his family name, I was happy to lend a hand to this worthy project.

While I do not know whether Fr. Sirico knew my friends Paul Ranieri and Vinny Palermo, his older brother Tony had to have known both of them. Tony Sirico played 'Paulie Walnuts' on the television series, the 'Sopranos.' This character was based on the life of my friend Paul; and the character of Tony Soprano, played by James Gandolfini, was based on the life of Vinny Palermo.

As an Italian-Catholic from our neighborhood who had reputedly worked for Joe Colombo and was a serious actor, I suspect Tony

Sirico knew both of them and that psychologically he would have been inclined to think a lot like both of them. Like Joe Colombo, all three were quick-witted and shrewd—had some degree of organizational and moral prudence.

Also, unlike the portrayal often given of reputedly 'organized-crime members' from my neighborhood, I doubt that Tony Sirico ever 'tended' to be a bully. While some sociopaths did exist among them, my experience was that these were the exception, not the norm. Someone Mafia connected in Brooklyn did not go around terrorizing old ladies and men, raping women, and abusing children.

Brooklyn 'Wise Guys' tended seriously to hurt—even kill—people who did that. They tended to hate bullies and people who disrespected the weak—especially immigrants like many of them, their parents, or relatives. Insulting or talking disparagingly about a person's mother in my neighborhood was anathema. A person who did that rarely escaped from a beating.

In most cases, these supposedly psychologically disposed criminals were also inclined to hate people who did not tell the truth to people they thought deserved to know the truth. They expected someone to be 'a stand-up guy'—someone who was not a 'Rat' or a hypocrite and could be trusted.

In being so psychologically inclined, they were following a first principle of 'Brooklyn Existentialism' and 'natural law,' which states that, "All human beings naturally love the truth." For this reason, all psychologically healthy human beings dislike, even hate, most of all the person who tells us the truth about ourselves when we know we are lying to ourselves about who or what we are.

Because the above depiction tended to be the psychological disposition my neighborhood's 'organized-crime leaders,' Dyker Heights was one of the safest places to live in New York City when I had lived there. This is so true that none of the members of my family would ever lock our doors when we left our house.

I think Fr. Sirico would likely agree with pretty much everything I have said above about the cultural psychology of the neighborhood leaders in Dyker Heights when we were young. I suspect, too, he would admit: (1) this psychology is a mental disposition he still has, and that (2) it has been a chief source of the organizational success he has achieved during his adult life.

Were he not to agree with what I said in the paragraph immediately above, he would have a difficult time explaining why, after his brother Tony had passed away in 2022, Fr. Sirico had no feeling of uneasiness or qualms of conscience presiding at a funeral Mass for his brother held at the Basilica of Regina Pacis in our Bay Ridge neighborhood.

Analogous to Yankee Stadium being the 'House that Babe Ruth had built' in the Bronx, the 'Basilica of Regina Pacis' was the 'House of God that Joe Profaci built' in Brooklyn. As signs of this, as part of its beautiful 60' x 20' ceiling fresco painted by the great artist Ignatio La Russa are members of the Profaci family.

And one of the most prized possessions and famous works of art—which was donated to it by parishioners after World War II—was a statue of the Virgin Mary adorned with 2 golden crowns made from wedding rings, necklaces, other forms of jewelry, and precious stones. At the request of the pastor, parishioners had given this crown as a token of thanksgiving for the safe return of their sons and daughters after the War.

This statue became especially famous in New York and nationwide after a thief had stolen its 2 crowns. After eight days of praying for its safe return, a package with the crowns 'miraculously' appeared at the Church rectory. Shortly thereafter, the thief who reputedly stole it—and was sorely lacking in neighborhood common sense—was discovered shot dead.

As part of the homily he gave for his brother, Fr. Sirico said, "If Paulie Walnuts can steal Heaven, so can you and I." Apart from his well-known humility, I think one reason Fr. Sirico included himself as one of the individuals who might be able to steal his way into Heaven was because, by his own public admission, like his brother, he was somewhat of a hellion in his younger days.

For example, about himself he has reported that, before he was 20 years old, around the start of the 1970s, he had publicly declared he was a homosexual and had left the Catholic Church to become a Protestant, Pentecostal Church minister in Seattle, Washington. In 1972, he affiliated his Church with the Metropolitan Community Church (MCC), which "had been founded in 1968 as the world's first church group with a primary ministry to gays, lesbian, bisexual, and transgender persons." In addition, during the 1970s, he became a proponent of same-sex marriage; and conducted the first such marriage in the history of Colorado, in Denver in 1975.

By his own admission, he was a child of the 1960s and was a card-carrying Leftist. About his personal journey that caused him to move from there to become founder of the Acton Institute, he has said:

"I suppose the fact that I spent time on the left of the political spectrum isn't the surprising thing. I'm a New Yorker; I'm a child of the '60s; I went to seminary during the early 1980s, when a baptized form of Marxism was next to godliness. When you take all that into account, my sojourn on the left has all about it almost the inevitability of the Marxist dialectic. What most people find surprising isn't that I was once a card-carrying lefty but that, despite my background, I somehow ended up as a defender of the free economy, of liberty, and limited government, of a traditional understanding of culture and morality, of all those things that America's Founders held dear and that our country is now in danger of losing."

In addition, regarding what had motivated him to establish the Acton Institute, he has stated: "The essential thing was my frustration when I was in seminary . . . to hear homilies preached that insulted business people. I knew this was a serious error, both theologically and pastorally. Theologically, because of the moral bankruptcy of socialism as an ideology. But pastorally because it alienated good people who were working and attempting to participate in the Christian mission."[1]

While, despite his background, it might be true that what most people might find surprising to learn about him was that Fr. Sirico wound up eventually becoming a defender of free economy, liberty, limited government, and a traditional understanding of morality and culture—"of all those things that America's Founders held dear

---

[1] See Fr. Sirico's Wikipedia biography at: https://en.wikipedia.org/wiki/Robert_Sirico

and that our country is now in danger of losing"—this outcome comes as no surprise whatsoever to me!

Next to family, 'respect' for workers, business people, and "all those things America's Founders held dear" were considered to be sacred truths and essential principles of common sense to anyone who was raised in our Dyker Heights neighborhood when we were young. And insulting any of them would have been like insulting somebody's mother—an action that defied common sense that would have merited a beating.

That this was the essential thing an Italian-American Catholic raised around Dyker Heights could not psychologically tolerate—the last that would finally break his back as a culturally ingrained 'Brooklyn Existentialist,' 'Philosophical Paladin,' and 'Samurai Thomist'—would be for some academic airhead with no street-smarts to insult hard-working business people should come as no surprise to anyone, including Fr. Sirico.

# Meditation Installment 14

*'Brooklyn Existentialism,' Michael Novak, Business as a Calling, Manichaeism, Greed, Duty, Honor, Conscience, and Public Shaming*

In the biographical reference to Fr. Sirico I cited in Installment 13, I intentionally omitted that, in that online source ('Wikipedia'), Fr. Sirico had expressly referred to reading a book on economics penned in 1982 by the famous, former 'darling-later-turned-traitor' of the political Left: Michael Novak (r.i.p), which had played a major role in Fr. Sirico abandoning the influence of the socialist Left on himself. In fact, he had directly cited Novak's 1982, Templeton-award-winning book—*The Spirit of Democratic Capitalism* (for which Michael had received a $1 million prize) as having been a turning point in: (1) his conversion from the failed economic policies of the socialist Left; and (2) causing his disgust for some of his theology teachers in seminary for disrespecting hard-working business people.

I did not cite this information about Novak then because, for a few reasons, I knew I had wanted to use it in this Installment 14.

One reason was that, since 1968, when I had entered the State University of New York at Buffalo (SUNY at Buffalo) as a Graduate Fellow and had joined the American Maritain Association (AMA), I was somewhat familiar with Novak's academic work. At the time, I had been reading his writings because I was aware of the influence that the famous French philosopher and student of St. Thomas Aquinas, Jacques Maritain, had had on Michael.

I was also aware at that time that Michael had been a speech writer for R. Sargent Schriver during the Kennedy administration, and that he had earlier coined the term 'The New Frontier,' which the Kennedy campaign had later adopted as one of its own.

During the 1980s, when I had worked organizing international conferences as Vice-president of the American Maritain Association and Michael had been named to hold the 'George Jewett Chair of Public Policy Research' at the American Enterprise Institute (AEI), Michael would graciously participate in sessions at these Maritain conferences without asking for any financial remuneration for so doing.

Sometime after 1986, when both of us had belonged to the Carnegie Council for Ethics in International Affairs, and Michael had started working as a U.S. ambassador to an extension of the 1975–1976 Helsinki Accords, I had asked him a question about diplomacy.

Based upon the behavior of Socrates as a shrewd psychologist in Plato's dialogues, I had become convinced that Socrates had used 'public shaming' as an essential first principle of his famous 'Socratic method' in practicing philosophy. When debating political Sophists like Thrasymachos and Callicles in the Athenian marketplace (*agora*, in Greek), for instance, he was constantly 'publicly shaming' them—diminishing audience respect for them—as an essential means of defeating their arguments and decreasing their negative influence on Athenian society.

I asked Michael whether he had ever found 'public shaming' to be a useful tool for diplomacy. His immediate response was a resounding "Yes"! In fact, he told me that this was exactly the technique the United States had finally resorted to after the Soviet Union had failed for more than 10 years to sign onto different parts of this agreement. Until they had started to shame the Soviets as part of a public opinion campaign, the United States had been unable to make any significant progress in getting a final agreement.

A second reason I made no mention in Installment 13 about Michael Novak's book *The Spirit of Democratic Capitalism* influencing Fr. Sirico was because, today, 'virtue shaming' is a rhetorical trick widely used by the political Left. They employ it because they realize that diminishing a person's reputation tends to undermine a person's public influence as someone to respect, honor, and trust. Undermining a good person's reputation for being trustworthy, in turn, decreases that person's ability to do good. Michael Novak had been one of the political Left's greatest defenders. Once he turned his back on them, they hated him—never lost an opportunity publicly to 'virtue shame' him. I wanted to bring this fact to the attention of readers of these Installments.

'Virtue shaming' was something organizational leaders in my Dyker Heights neighborhood repeatedly experienced— sometimes with good reason. Hence, they were always highly sensitive to anyone—especially their own relatives—publicly disrespecting and shaming them.

A third reason I did not mention in Installment 13 Novak's influence on Fr. Sirico was because I had wanted to add an explanation about why his seminary theology teachers had so grossly misunderstood the nature of democratic capitalism and had reduced it to 'crony capitalism.' They had mistakenly thought that, by nature, all business people, all capitalists, are essentially 'greedy.' Unwittingly, they were psychologically blinded by a tacit adherence to the ancient Christian heresies of Manichaeism and Pelagianism—which Fr. Sirico appears to have sensed, and instinctively recoiled against, at the time.

One motivation for Novak abandoning the failed policies of the socialist Left was that his reading of the Scottish philosopher of uncommon common sense, Adam Smith, had taught him that 'greed' could not explain the behavior of philanthropists like Andrew Carnegie. And, while Smith was not an overtly religious man, Novak was well aware that Smith had been a firm believer in the 'Invisible Hand' of Providence guiding human economic interaction for the greater good.

Another motivation for Novak jettisoning his prior economic ignorance had been his slowly increasing realization that 'leading the life of a business person can actually be a human vocation.' As a result, he later wrote a book entitled *Business as a Calling: Work and the Examined Life* (Simon & Schuster, Free Press: New York, 1996).

The businessmen from my Dyker Heights neighborhood were of the same mind. The organizational leaders of this group were theists, people with a conscience who tended never to lose total contact with reality. They had a sense of the 'Invisible Hand' of Providence guiding their lives. They also had a sense of duty, and felt they had a moral and professional responsibility to protect their family and neighbors—felt ashamed of themselves if they were not able to live up to this responsibility. They feared the wrath of God and were firm believers in the reality of Hell. Hence, along with many other of their

Brooklyn colleagues, they sought to be buried in 'a sacred place with blessed ground'—in a Catholic cemetery.

To verify the truth of the claim I made in the above paragraph, all one need do is take a look at the names of some of the community leaders, along with my mother and father, who are buried in St. John's Catholic Cemetery in Middle Village, Queens, New York: Salvatore D'Aquila, Carlo Gambino, Joseph Profaci, Joe Colombo, Vito Genovese, Carmine Galante, Salvatore Maranzano, Agniello ('The Hat') Dellacroce, Paul Vario, Salvatore (Charlie 'Lucky') Luciano, and John Gotti.

This is a burial location that, in 2022, along with other Catholic cemeteries, the United States Conference of Catholic Bishops implicitly had called "sacred places with blessed ground."

In closing this Installment, if you think these men buried in this cemetery were not somewhat good human beings, consider how they would have behaved had they been atheists with no conscience in touch with reality, no belief in divine Providence, no sense of duty, no fear of going to Hell, and had been totally deprived of the benefits of sanctifying grace!

# Meditation Installment 15

*How the 'Invisible Hand of Providence,' Senators JFK, RFK, Other 'Great Role Models,' and 'Camelot' Influenced Me to Become a 'Brooklyn Existentialist,' 'Philosophical Paladin,' and 'Samurai Thomist'*

Before talking about the above topics of the 'Invisible Hand of Providence,' Senators JFK and RFK, other great role models I have had, and Camelot, I want to preface what I say below by mentioning that, whenever I talk in these Installments about anyone as a 'Brooklyn Existentialist,' I am referring to a person who is a 'Philosophical Paladin' and 'Samurai Thomist.' The former term is interchangeable with these two subsequent terms.

That being said, I continue this Installment by noting that, after I had entered my Freshman year at Xaverian High School in Bay Ridge, Brooklyn, in the late afternoon of 27 October 1960—less than two weeks before he was elected President of the United States of America on 08 November 1960—I shook hands with Senator John F. Kennedy. Almost exactly 4 years later, in October 1964, I spoke with Robert F. Kennedy after he had delivered a talk on the steps of Spellman Hall at Iona College in New Rochelle, New York.

For some reason, as I raised my hand to ask him a question, to my surprise—even though many hands had been raised by members of the audience—he called on me. My question was about the Civil Rights Bill that was being hotly debated in Congress, but had not yet been passed.

I had wanted to find out from him what he thought about Barry Goldwater's opposition to the Bill because Goldwater had claimed the Bill was unnecessary. Goldwater's position was that he had opposed the Legislation because he thought it was unnecessary. All that was needed to secure minority rights in the United States, he said, was for laws already on the books to be enforced by the proper governmental agencies.

Despite the fact that RFK had dodged answering my question, I was impressed by the courteous way in which he had done so; and, from the way he had reacted to it—flashing that great Kennedy grin as if to tell me he was pleased I had asked it. He simply replied that he thought enforcing existing Legislation was not enough. He did not explain why it was not enough.

That I would shake hands with JFK on that afternoon was something I had never anticipated. In fact, prior to his running for the presidency, I do not think I had ever heard of him.

86th St. from Shore Road to Stillwell Ave. in Brooklyn runs for miles—at least 40 to 50 blocks. The famous car chase in the movie 'The French Connection' under the elevated train itself extended for 26 blocks. And John Travolta's famous movie 'Saturday Night Fever' was mostly filmed between 80th and 92nd Streets—much of it taking place between 86th St. and 4th Ave. to 86th St. and 22nd Ave.

When I was in grammar school and high school, as far as it stretched, by late afternoon every day, 86th St. was mobbed with shoppers and teenagers hanging out. The day I met JFK at the intersection of 86th St. and 4th Ave. was just one of those days—except that, as I was walking from 5th Ave. to 4th Ave., the number of people appeared to be much larger than normal. I could hear some of them talking about JFK—and some, not positively.

As I was moving along, I could also hear a loud-speaker system coming from a car blaring in the background from about a block behind me. The closer I got to 4th Ave., the more difficult became my ability to navigate my way down the street. To do so I had to get closer to the curb.

By the time I had reached the intersection, as Senator Kennedy's Chevrolet convertible was rounding the corner with its top down, the sheer bulk of the crowd pressing against me pushed me off the curb just as JFK (looking like a movie star, with a full head of reddish-brown hair, pearly white teeth, and deep blue eyes) leaned out of the backseat, flashed a great smile at me, and extended his hand to me—which I immediately shook.

From that day onward, a conviction I had had in elementary school that God, or the 'Invisible Hand of Providence,' was: (1) 'guiding and protecting me' and (2) 'calling me' to do some kind of good with my life became even stronger. After I had spoken to RFK at Iona, this conviction was reinforced.

In part, I had had this entrenched mindset early on because, even then, I had realized I was living an exceptionally fortunate life. I had been raised in idyllic circumstances, surrounded by good and talented people who, knowingly or not, were constantly enhancing the quality of my life.

Apart from some of the people I have already mentioned in these Installments, as great role models I had Brooklyn Dodger players like Pee Wee Reese, Carl Erskine, Duke Snider, Clem Labine,

Preacher Roe, Sandy Koufax, Jackie Robinson, Gil Hodges, and Roy Campanella.

Before I had entered grammar school, Clem Labine and his family had lived on my block for a short time, and I used to play with his son Clem Jr. (aka, 'Jay'). Preacher Roe and his family had lived around the block from me on 81st St. I used to play with his son, Tommy. And Pee Wee Reese, Carl Erskine, and Duke Snider had lived within about a 12 block radius of me in Bay Ridge.

During and after his short presidency, the years in which JFK had served were often referred to as a time of 'Camelot.' As I grew older, I started to realize that I have been living my whole life in a time and place like 'Camelot.'

Looking back on these years, I have come to realize that 'the reality' of Divine Providence and of the existence of a benevolent God is evident. I have no doubt whatsoever about this reality. Furthermore, even though he is famous for having presented 5 ways of demonstrating the existence of God by showing how different realities evident to our senses (like motion and beings coming into existence and going out of existence) are only rationally explicable if what he calls 'God' exists, St. Thomas Aquinas was not presenting these arguments to convince himself that God exists (*Summa theologiae*, 1, q. 2, a. 3, respondeo).

He accepted the existence of God as an evident truth! While he believed in God and God's existence in the sense that he 'trusted' God not to lie or deceive him, he did not believe in the existence of God any more than does a person who sees that a building is on fire 'believe' it is on fire. In this sense of the word, we cannot believe what we evidently know! Neither could Aquinas.

I am of the same mindset. Furthermore, this is an evident first principle for anyone who is a 'Brooklyn Existentialist.'

# Meditation Installment 16

*How JFK and RFK had Enkindled in Me the Idea of Becoming a Professional Politician and Why, by the Late 1960s, I had Abandoned this Idea*

Before returning to talk further about my grammar school years as largely idyllic, and about friends I had known during this time, in this Installment I want to explain: (1) how JFK and RFK had influenced me to contemplate becoming a professional politician and (2) why, even though at the time I had no doubt I could have been elected to high political office in New York City, and even nationally, before the end of the 1960s, I had soured on realizing this idea.

Actually, even before coming in contact with JFK and RFK, given the many politically influential contacts my father had within Dyker Heights, Bay Ridge, and Bensonhurst, I had known I could easily have done quite well in local and national politics. In and of itself, my father's close friendship with Judge Ross DiLorenzo could have guaranteed me a lucrative career in professional politics.

For those not familiar with Ross DiLorenzo, during the 1960s, he was a political powerhouse, kingmaker, within the Democrat Party comparable to Meade Esposito. He lived 4 blocks from me (on 84th St., and 11th Ave.), 2 blocks from Tony Anastasia (aka, Anastasio; on 82nd St. and 11th Ave.). Vinny Palermo lived in between them (on 83rd St., between 10th and 11th Ave.).

Like my father, Judge DiLorenzo had attended New Utrecht High School. After this, he went to Georgetown University and graduated from Georgetown Law School. Among his many achievements, in 1966, he helped organize, and became President of, the Italian-American Anti-Defamation League—of which Frank Sinatra became National Chairman.

Well-known to anyone familiar with JFK's presidency are the following 2 short sentences from his inaugural address delivered on 20 January 1961: "Ask not what your country can do for you. Ask what you can do for your country."

As a 'Brooklyn Existentialist,' these two sentences could not help but resonate in my ears as a 'Providential Calling'—a moral duty (*officium*, in the words of Marcus Tullius Cicero) to which I would later see St. Thomas Aquinas refer toward the start of his *Summa contra gentiles*. They were calling me to become the same sort of 'Philosophical Paladin' and 'Samurai Thomist' that JFK and RFK were.

Even though during my high school years (1959–1963) I had been thinking about pursuing a military career after graduating from college, the assassinations of RFK and JFK combined with other events had convinced me, before the end of the 1960s, to abandon that idea and that of becoming a professional politician.

Before I had graduated from high school, I had injured my left knee running track. During my college years (1963—1967), I had dislocated the same knee several times and had weakened it to the point that I knew I could not pass a military physical. As a result, I abandoned my idea of a military career.

As far as pursuing a political career, aside from the assassinations of JFK and RFK turning me off to that notion, coming into contact with: (1) the teachings of Socrates in Plato's dialogues (especially in the *Apology*) related to the essentially corrupt nature of professional politicians and (2) the lies I had witnessed in the mainstream media—especially in the 'New York Times'—about 'mostly peaceful' protests against the War 'being mostly violent,' caused me to abandon that idea.

The propaganda supporting the War nauseated me so much that, even now at my advanced age, being in the presence of a professional politician physically upsets my stomach, makes me feel like puking,

Because my brother Bob was a U.S. Marine and I did not want publicly to embarrass him or my father, I never participated in anti-War protests in college. At the same time, I made my views known to my brother and my father. Neither one was very happy with me at the time. In fact, among other things, because I had grown a beard, my father was concerned that I was turning into a political Leftist.

My father never told me about this concern, but I heard about it from two of his friends ('Cheech' and 'Blackie') at a retirement dinner given for him toward the start of the 1970s at the John Hughes Council K of C—an event for which I had shaved off my beard. At that time, Cheech said to me: "I'm glad to see you've turned out OK, Kid. Your 'Fodder' was worried about you turning into 'a hippie.'

While that never happened, as I will continue to talk about in subsequent Installments, a love for the uncommon commonsense teachings of Socrates, Plato, Aristotle, and St. Thomas Aquinas increasingly solidified my philosophical nature as a 'Brooklyn Existentialist.'

# Meditation Installment 17

*4 Evident First Principles, Truths, and Definitions a 'Brooklyn existentialist' Understands Early in Life about the Nature of Being a Leader, Leadership, an Organization, and Being an Organizational Leader*

Four of the first, evident principles, truths, and definitions a 'Brooklyn Existentialist' learns as a youth are general (or generic) ones about the nature of: (1) leadership, (2) being a leader, (3) organizations, and (4) being an organizational leader.

The first of these generic principles/truth/and definitions is that, 'strictly speaking,' leadership is essentially a species of communications activity. Specifically, it is an activity that consists in what some people today call a 'meeting of minds.' Because of its complicated nature—which I will attempt immediately to explain—I prefer to refer to this as a 'meeting of psychologies.'

When I say a 'Brooklyn Existentialist' 'learns' these principles as a youth, I do not mean that he or she learns them through formal, academic instruction. I mean he or she acquires them by 'psychological insight'—immediate understanding, induction—usually at home. If not at home, generally he or she acquires some understanding of them in a less peaceful setting.

Like any good 'Brooklyn Existentialist' would do, chiefly and 'strictly speaking,' generically I define 'leadership' as 'an act of induction, insight, that communicates to a follower or followers a mutual-understanding of an essentially existing superiority/inferiority relationship existing between a stronger and weaker being.' In a wider sense, 'leadership' can also refer to such a relationship existing as a virtue, habit, or disposition.

By the immediately preceding definition, I mean that 'leadership is a communication of mutual understanding' between at least 2 people, or between at least one human being and an animal that, in some way, one of the two, or more, is more powerful than the other(s).

Implied in my use of the terms 'insight' and 'induction' in my definition of 'leadership' and a 'leader' is some understanding on the part of a follower or followers which—by means of commonsense shrewdness, animal instinct, or prudence—makes immediately evident to the follower(s) that his, her, or their health, safety, and/or life essentially depends upon his, her, or their ability to accept the reality to this superior/inferior relationship.

When I say a 'Brooklyn Existentialist' first 'learns' this evident truth, I do not mean that this is a verbally communicated truth. This communication need have nothing to do with speaking, reasoning, or persuading by argument. 'Strictly speaking,' we are never persuaded by verbal communication, or by any communication just by itself. 'Human beings are only persuaded by inductive understanding—or by our own misunderstanding that we mistakenly judge to be understanding—of an attempted communication.'

To be persuaded, a person must say to himself for herself: (1) 'I understand what is being communicated to me'; and (2) 'what is being communicated to me to do or not to do makes common sense to me.' Furthermore, I must understand (or mistakenly understand)

# Meditation Installment 17

this with all of my psychological faculties (intellect, will, senses, and emotions) and agree to accept it with all the same faculties!

'Strictly speaking,' understanding—or misunderstanding mistaken as understanding (being on the wrong page, with someone else in a mutual attempt to communicate)—always precedes any and every form of reasoning and act of persuasion. 'Leadership' and 'being a leader' in this sense need have nothing to do with 'verbal' communication.

By communicating mutual understanding, leaders and leadership communicate to followers a receptivity to take direction from leaders by overcoming any resistance from followers to do so. Leadership is simply a 'Communication of Mutual Understanding' (CMU) that, some-how, leaders are able to convey to followers.

The means leaders use to 'deliver this message' can consist in simply being, or appearing to be: drop-dead gorgeous or handsome; rich; in great physical shape; famous; politically or socially connected, and so on. It can also consist in some form of body language, such as walking in some way—for example, with a confident, military gait—or in something as simple as a smirk or a smile; raising an eyebrow; pointing a finger; or ignoring someone.

In my Dyker Heights neighborhood, it might consist in mailing someone a dead fish wrapped in a newspaper. In a local law court, it might involve bringing a relative to sit in a courtroom during a jury trial; or having the court clerk stand next to you talking to you and smiling at the traffic court judge who is supposed to determine whether or not to fine you for a traffic violation.

Human leaders are chiefly behavioral psychologists. They have an exceptional understanding of real human nature, and of how to incline other people to listen to, and take direction from, them.

In addition to being great behavioral psychologists, great organizational leaders have excellent insight into: (1) identifying individuals who possess or lack the precise qualities needed to execute an action—get a job done—in the individual situation; (2) being able to get the right individuals to work with and for them as members of a team; and (3), like a great orchestra leader, harmonize qualities of team members, as perfectly as possible, to execute really doable deeds needed to be done in an individual situation.

Organizational leaders in my Dyker Heights neighborhood were masters in all the above forms of psychology.

# Meditation Installment 18

*Further Meditation on How a 'Brooklyn Existentialist' Conveys 'Communication of Mutual Understanding' (CMU) of Being a Leader' to Followers—and Especially to New Ones*

In this Installment, I continue my reflection that the way in which a 'Brooklyn Existentialist' leader starts to convey to a new follower that he or she is a 'leader' is never by entering into a debate or discussion with a follower about the nature of leadership, or about whether this or that person in this situation should be a leader. It is by immediately causing a follower to understand that every interaction between two human beings: (1) is organizational; (2) exists within an organization of somewhat social unequals; and (3) starts a new organization of social unequals within that already existing organization.

A 'Brooklyn Existentialist' leader immediately conveys to a new follower that, when human beings start to communicate with each other, we do so as human beings—not as plants, brute animals, or angels—existing in a specific time and place. That is, we do so within a new situation, under a different set of circumstances that constitute the start of a new organization.

'Brooklyn Existentialists' always understand that, when they start to communicate with a new follower, they do so like a seasoned salesperson does with a new customer. They first have to qualify that customer to see whether or not that customer is 'follower-worthy' (worthy of being a follower and long-term customer in their organization). If they do not do this, they realize their communication will not be productive for them or the customer.

Unhappily for them, followers entering a new organization quite often do not understand that they have done so, like new customers. Nevertheless, they have entered into an unfamiliar organization in the form of a situation in which they are not in charge. And, having made this mistake, sometimes they compound this error by behaving as if they are in charge. Not every customer is always right.

When a seasoned 'Brooklyn Existentialist' leader confronts such a situation, he or she immediately knows how to clarify it by talking nicely,' 'respectfully,' to this prospective follower in a language that he or she understands. He does not give him or her a 'knuckle sandwich.' Because they seriously lack prudence, this is what bad leaders do.

In contrast, a 'Brooklyn Existentialist' leader communicates to new followers that he or she is the one who is communicating to them in no uncertain terms the 'mutual understanding' that he or she is in charge. The new follower contributes nothing to this initial mutual understanding.

While a 'Brooklyn Existentialist' will convey to a new follower that the leader expects a follower to give some respectful resistance to an organizational leader if a decision a leader is making might hurt the organization, such resistance does not include the follower mistakenly thinking that he or she is the organizational leader, or that he or she is entering a debate about the nature of this mutual understanding. The leader, not the follower, articulates and communicates the mutual understanding.

'Brooklyn Existentialist' leaders are good leaders. Because they naturally incline to make the smart choice, in the individual situation they naturally incline to make the right choice. Since the right choice is always the prudent choice, as best they can, they attempt to make the prudent decision.

After I had returned to college teaching in Staten Island, New York, where I had a lot of students in class from my old Brooklyn neighborhood, I realized that, when I started a course, I had to communicate to my new followers the 'mutual understanding' that I was the organizational leader of a new crew. To do this, starting on day one, I would begin to qualify students to determine whether or not they were qualified to take my course.

This was not difficult for me to do. On the first day, pretty much by looking at the class and the way students in it initially behaved, I could pretty much determine which students I could teach and which ones would be wasting their time and money, and my energy, taking my course.

As a 'Brooklyn Existentialist,' I recognized I had a moral duty to encourage unqualified students not to take my class for the simple reason that they were not likely to succeed in it. Two things made my ability to succeed in fulfilling my moral duty exceptionally difficult. A third thing, however, made it very easy.

One difficulty I encountered was that university registrars do not chiefly tend to focus their attention on having a moral duty and professional responsibility to protect the welfare of students. Their chief concern tends to be 'to put asses in classes.' At St. John's University during this time, this meant enrolling at least 30 students in each required course I taught.

This imprudent disposition on their part was complicated by an equally imprudent disposition on the part of many students. Their chief concern was to take whatever course they were required to take at the time they wanted to take it.

These twofold acts of imprudence required me, for the first month of each new required course, to give as many tests as I could, which I knew unqualified students would fail. In this way, by the end of the month, I had a group of students in my course who possessed the virtue of *docilitas* (teachability).

One thing, however, made my job especially easy. I knew I was from the same neighborhood as many of my students.

So, on the first day of class, I would tell them they could not avoid the work I required of them because, "Whoever you know, I know." I would add that they had to fulfill the assignments I was giving them. If they did not, I might contact someone in their family to encourage them to do so.

My classes at St. John's at the time had an unusual mix of students. Starting around 1980, the Archdiocese of New York began sending nuns and seminarians to St. John's to take some required courses in theology and philosophy. Since I was one of the teachers they had been recommended to take, I would often have several of them in the same class with students who had easily recognizable names in Brooklyn and Staten Island. For example, in one class I had some nuns and priests studying together with students with the following surnames: 'Gambino,' 'Castellano,' and 'Capone.'

While, for some time, I think some students doubted the veracity of what I was telling them about my knowing anyone they knew, within a short time I had the good fortune of having a student enroll in my course who was named 'Paul Ranieri' (the same name as that of my friend Paul, aka, 'Paulie Walnuts'). Before the class had started, the registrar would email a course list with the photo and some background information about each student in the class. The photo of the 'Paul Ranieri' in my class was the spitting image of my friend Paul.

With this information in hand, on the first day of class in which I encountered the student Paul Ranieri, after I had just finished telling the class that I was from the local area and that they should not give me a hard time because anyone they knew I knew, I turned to look at Paul. He was sitting in the front of the class, to my right, in the last row by a window. As I looked at him, I noticed he was fingering a ring on his right hand that I recognized had belonged to his father. It was not my friend Paul's 'Wolf-ring.' It was gold, with his father's initials on it.

Immediately, I said: "Paul, how is your Uncle Charlie, Charlie Fiumano, doing? Is he still living down in South Jersey? I see you're wearing your father's ring. How is he doing? If I tell you I am a close friend of your father, and if what I say is true, would you recommend that other students take me seriously about my knowing anyone they know, that they should not give me a hard time in class, and that they should do what I tell them to do?"

Looking at me somewhat dumbfounded and amazed, Paul's short, but forceful, reply was, "Oh, yes, I would!

In a nutshell, this short conversation I had with Paul in class is an example of the way in which a 'Brooklyn Existentialist' leader respectfully and nicely conveys communication of mutual understanding about who is actually leading an organization to new followers in a new situation.

# Meditation Installment 19

*Gilson, the Decline of the West, and the Nature of Man as a 'Rational Animal'*

As far back as 1967, when I first entered the Graduate Philosophy Department at the State University of New York at Buffalo (SUNY, Buffalo) and read Étienne Gilson's masterful 1937 monograph *The Unity of Philosophical Experience* (published by Charles Scribner's Sons), I have been held under the sway of the content of its penultimate Chapter XI, entitled, "The Breakdown of Modern Philosophy." To me this chapter marks the crescendo of Gilson's analysis of the history of Western philosophy as an account of the West as a culture unique in world history. This is because Western culture is the only culture in the world where its institutions essentially grew out of its unwavering cultural adherence to the evident first principle and understanding that 'man is a rational animal'!

When he wrote this book, Gilson had no doubt that, like him, many of his readers were aware that, culturally, for some time, the West had been declining. He also had no doubt that this decline had been chiefly due to one fact. An idea and ideal of man as 'a rational animal'—which he dubbed 'The Western Creed'—had been an unwavering conviction and essential first principle holding the West together since the ancient Greek philosophers. According to him, however, the French Revolution marked the time when some leading Western intellectuals had started to feel something was wrong with this first principle.

Since he and his readers were the bearer of Western culture, Gilson stated the West "cannot be dying, and dying in us, without our being aware of it." Shortly after making this evident observation, he asked the following sobering question: "Can a social order, begotten by a common faith in the value of certain principles, keep on living when all faith in these be principles is lost?"

Immediately after doing this, he started to illustrate what he understood to be implications of that question by giving a summary description of 'The Western Creed' in light of its two fundamental principles.

The first of these principles is an evident conviction that all human beings have an "eminent dignity." Not only did the ancient Greeks never waiver in the conviction that, "of all things that can be found in nature, man is by far the highest" and most important for us all to know. Gilson was convinced that the ancient Greek cultural principle of self-knowledge ('Know thyself') is more than the key to understanding Greek culture. It is the key to understanding the classical culture of the Western world—that is, of the Western world from the ancient Greeks to the beginning of the 20th century!

The second of these principles is 'a definite conviction that reason is man's specific difference. Man is best described as a rational animal; deprive man of reason, and what is left is animal, not man.' The reason man is best described as a 'rational animal,' therefore, is because "the rational nature of man is the only conceivable foundation for a rational system of ethics. Morality is essentially normality; for a rational being to act and to behave either without reason, or contrary to its dictates is to act and behave, not exactly as a beast, but as a beastly man, which is worse... because that means the complete oblivion of his own nature, and hence his final destruction."

In fact, according to Gilson, "Western culture is dying wherever it" (that is, 'this principle') has been forgotten." If this statement of Gilson was true close to 90 years ago, as some colleagues of mine and I had realized decades ago, this meant that: (1) even at that time, all the West's cultural institutions and wherever the influence of Western culture and its institutions had spread (that is, the entire world and its institutions) was collapsing! And (2) the situation had become even worse in our time.

No wonder, then, should exist why, about 25 years ago, colleagues of mine and I started to reflect on the global loss of common sense and the need to restore it. We did so because, contained within Gilson's above identification of morality with 'human normality' is that, in some way, being a 'rational animal' consists essentially in being a 'prudent animal,' and behaving as such—as an animal with common sense. Saying that man is a 'rational animal' is not enough, however, if what we mean by a 'rational animal' is an animal that simply reasons, or is reduced to a logical animal.

To restore the West and the world to common and uncommon commonsense sanity, we have to be as precise as possible about the nature of human and philosophical rationality. We can start doing so by observing that, on the first page of his "Foreword" to *The Unity of Philosophical Experience*, Gilson had described the history of philosophy he was writing to be a history of "the nature of philosophical knowledge itself"—that is, with philosophy being a way, or 'method,' of knowing in the sense of being a psychological attempt to understand what we think are evident, internal causes, or first principles, existing within 'things' (within what I call 'organizations,' or 'organizational wholes') to make intelligible the behavior, or action, of these things.

What I am saying is so true that, toward the end of his Chapter II (which he entitles, "Theologism and Philosophy"), Gilson states:

"I sometimes wonder how many similar experiments will be necessary before men acquire some philosophical experience. A certain man adopts a certain attitude" (by 'attitude,' Gilson means a psychological disposition or habit of applying principles of understanding) "in philosophy, and he follows it consistently, until he finds himself face to face with unwelcome consequences. He does his best to dodge them, but his own disciples, beginning as they do just where the master stopped, have less scruples than he about letting his principles publicly confess their necessary consequences. Everybody then realizes that the only way to get rid of those consequences is to shift the philosophical position from which they spring." (By shifting "the philosophical position from which they spring," Gilson means psychologically deciding to get rid of the philosophical principles being used—which do not work—or to change the way they are being used).

"Then the school dies; but it is not unlikely that one or two centuries later, in some university whence history has been banished as harmful to philosophical originality, some young man, still blessed with his native ignorance, will discover a similar position. As he will live and write in another time, he will say very old things in a new way. Yet they will be old; his philosophy will be stillborn and neither he nor his disciples will ever be able to quicken it. The trouble is that once philosophers fail, their disheartened supporters never blame their master; they blame it on philosophy itself. 'There' begins the straight road that leads to conscious and openly declared skepticism."

Clearly, in his Chapter II, Gilson is describing the essential nature of a moron and oxymoron: an imprudent philosopher (a fool, someone lacking in common sense as an organizational, behavioral psychologist). Anyone with common sense evidently understands that, if the principles you are using do not help you to understand the behavior of something, something is wrong with the principles you are employing or the way you are employing them. Such being the case, anyone with a modicum of common sense would change his or her behavior. He or she would not continue repeatedly to make the same mistake ad infinitum. *Verbum sat sapienti.*

In my next Installment, I plan to consider how meditating about the nature of 'Brooklyn Existentialism' enabled me finally to understand the precise nature of man as a 'rational animal' and how such an animal tends to behave within an individual situation.

# Meditation Installment 20

*How Meditating about the Nature of 'Brooklyn Existentialism' Enabled Me Finally to Understand the Nature of Man as a 'Rational Animal' and How Such an Animal Behaves within the Individual Situation*

To some extent, almost everything I meditate about in this Installment I have already discussed in previous ones. I cover these now in a somewhat different way because years of teaching experience have made evident to me that advancement in learning becomes easier to the extent that we periodically review, and talk about somewhat differently, what we have come to know about a subject. Prior knowledge is always a first principle of more perfectly learning and understanding what we already know.

As Gilson well understood, philosophy, science, is always and everywhere a way of knowing. Philosophy, science, does not begin with reasoning. It starts with knowing in the form of understanding. That this claim is true is easy to show. Anyone who disagrees with it would have to know, understand, what the claim is before he or she could reasonably disagree with it. Otherwise, he or she would not know, understand, with what he or she is disagreeing—which is what many university professors often do nowadays.

Contrary to the way university philosophy professors practice philosophy today, a 'Brooklyn Existentialist' always starts philosophizing with induction—immediate understanding. If we understand nothing, we can reason about nothing.

Furthermore, when we reason, we can only reason in one of two ways: (1) from effect to cause or (2) from cause to effect.

Reasoning from effect to cause is 'analysis,' or reasoning 'analytically.' Reasoning from cause to the effect is 'synthesis'—reasoning 'synthetically,' or from beginning principle(s) to an end principle (conclusion).

I describe these forms of reasoning as proceeding from a beginning 'principle' to an end 'principle' or from an end 'principle' to a beginning 'principle' because, 'strictly speaking' a 'principle' is the starting point: that from which some motion, action, or way of being proceeds. In this respect, the starting line and the finish line of a race are its beginning and end principles.

When we reason analytically, we divide, or break up, an organizational whole (end principle)—something bigger, or more general—into its constituent parts (or principles)—something smaller. When we reason synthetically, we unite constituent parts—something smaller, or specific, into an organizational whole—something bigger, or general.

Classical logicians call analytical reasoning 'deductive' and synthetic reasoning 'inductive.' By 'deductive' reasoning, they understand themselves to be moving a person's focus of intellectual attention (what a person is intellectually paying attention to) from *an understanding of* a beginning premise (proposition, or term) through *an understanding of* a middle premise (proposition, or term) to *an understanding of* a concluding premise (proposition or term). Inductive reasoning just reverses the process.

Crucial to note about moving the focus of human attention in the way such logicians do is that it has as its chief aim moving from one understanding, through another understanding, to a concluding or beginning understanding. That is, the chief goal of the classical logician is to provide people with a method for producing future understanding from prior understanding through an intermediary understanding—or what logicians call the middle 'premise' or 'term' of a syllogism.

Considered in this way, the middle term of a syllogism is a middle cause—an essential means to an end—in a reasoning process. While students and professors very often consider this syllogistic act of logic to be totally abstract, and in no way concrete, practical, or productive, understood in the way that an ancient philosopher like Aristotle or a medieval theologian like St. Thomas Aquinas understood it, syllogistic logic is an art, is mainly a practical and productive activity. Its chief goal is to use understanding to 'produce' understanding.

Related to a 'Brooklyn Existentialist's' understanding of the nature of a human being as a 'rational animal,' this productive nature of syllogistic logic is crucial to recognize. A 'Brooklyn Existentialist's' chief focus of attention in philosophy is on understanding unity and action—on understanding how to build, maintain, unite, divide, and destroy organizational action in the individual circumstance, or situation (circumstance and situation being identical). This is a major quality that makes a 'Brooklyn Existentialist' radically different from all other species of philosopher.

In the individual situation or circumstance, possessing the virtue of prudence is a necessary condition for immediately 'seeing,' 'intuiting,' 'inducing,' 'emotionally sensing' the middle term of a practical or productive syllogism—the means to the end here and now! It is a quality any good pool player uses to put just the right amount of 'English' on a cue ball to direct another ball into a pocket on a pool table. It is also the same sort of quality a golfer uses when putting a golf ball with just the right amount of intensity to sink it into a cup.

In this respect, prudence integrates in the present all the psychological and physical faculties of a human being. When practiced habitually related to healthy and unhealthy, physical and psychological activities, it produces a perfectly integrated person: a person with 'integrity,' 'character.'

In prior Installments, I have noted how the virtue of prudence is more than the form of all virtue. It is the source (proximate first principle and cause) *of our commonsense understanding* of shrewdness, quick-wittedness, honor, duty, and of a healthy conscience (which puts us in touch, and maintains for us contact, with sense reality).

Recall that prudence is chiefly located in 'particular' or 'cogitative reason'—in what St. Thomas refers to as the 'animal part of the soul.' Therein, prudence is analogous to instinct in brute animals. According to St. Thomas, being a prudent animal *is* the specific difference that makes a human being a 'rational animal.' It is also the first principle out of which grows the whole of philosophy and science properly understood.

Recall, also, that, in brute animals, instinct (the estimative sense) serves as the essential means through which, via the irascible emotions of hope and fear, these animals sense utility and non-utility, safety and danger, species-friends and enemies. In addition, in so doing, these animals employ a form of immediate understanding analogous to the commonsense human understanding achieved by means of an 'enthymeme.' They immediately induce the means to an end.

This function of the irascible emotions, or passions, of fear, and hope distinguish them in nature from the emotions, passions, of our pleasure-seeking (concupiscible) appetite. This unique quality of the emotions, passions, of hope and fear is something crucial to understand in order to be able to live a happy life.

The emotions, passions, of hope and fear enable us to 'sense' real good and evil in the individual circumstance. In conjunction with a healthy intellectual faculty and a good will, they enable us to develop the respect for honor, duty, and a healthy conscience that transform us from instinct-driven animals into morally decent human beings.

In contrast, in and of themselves, the pleasure-seeking emotions, passions, can produce none of these goods in us. In and of themselves, they are blind to these goods. For this reason, a person who reduces the pursuit of human happiness to the pursuit of pleasure is doomed to be miserable—to live the life of an intemperate fool.

Plato is well-known for maintaining that nothing is worse than for a fool to get what he wants. I disagree. Something is worse: to live a life in which every decision, choice, a person makes is one dictated by a fool and coming to the realization that you are that fool!

As I have previously noted, I compare the form of immediate understanding that involves *inducing the middle term of a syllogism* to that of the key ingredient used by a salesman as part of an 'elevator pitch.' I have also indicated that business people with common sense tend to get annoyed with colleagues who have to engage in all premises of a syllogistic argument to try to persuade someone to do something. They tend to view such colleagues as having no business common sense.

Such people would also annoy friends from my youth in Dyker Heights—like Paul and Vinny—who would tend immediately to express their annoyance with them by throwing them down a flight of stairs.

In part, I recall these points above about the similarity between commonsense human behavior and healthy animal instinct because I have lived my life in close proximity to more than a few people who suffered from one or more forms of psychological difficulty.

For example, for 10 years, while at St. John's University in Staten Island, New York, I was the Assistant Director of the University's prison program. Several of my students were incarcerated for major crimes. One was head of the Chinese Mafia in New York City. Another was one of the most dangerous people I have ever met in my life—in prison for killing several drug dealers, who were stealing money from him. Both helped save my life when the prefabricated building in which we were conducting class was accidentally set on fire after an inmate had decided to burn a mattress in another prisoner's cell because he was unhappy with an administrative decision to place this person near to him.

For several years, I also taught inmates at Rikers Island Maximum Security Correctional Facility in Queens, NY. While doing so, I gave a one-time guest lecture to inmates in full lockup there about the nature of Western philosophy, and how it had originated with the ancient Greeks. Around this same time, for 5 years I drove taxi part-time on weekends in Manhattan.

Throughout these hazardous situations, because of my training as a 'Brooklyn Existentialist' and protection by Divine Providence, I never suffered any major physical or psychological damage. In this Installment I have mentioned the physical and psychological health and safety benefits that becoming a 'Brooklyn Existentialist' provides to be a unique good that will dramatically improve the quality of anyone's life. Because, so far as I know, no reader of these meditations will be able to acquire this good anywhere else, I hope you will be prudent enough to take advantage of the opportunity of doing so now. Making this prudent choice might someday save your life. At the very least, it should somewhat improve it.

# Meditation Installment 21

*On the Nature of Man as a 'Prudent Animal,' the Integral, or Constituent, Parts of Prudence, and How the Virtue of Prudence Helps a Person Become a 'Master,' not a 'Victim,' of Circumstances*

In my next Installment I plan to give readers a break from focusing attention on psychological principles and qualities of human nature and behavior and return to talking about some unconventional and colorful characters I knew during my youth. Because being: (1) a prudent animal is *the* specific difference that makes a human being a rational animal; and (2) the nature of being a rational animal enters into every human action—gives every human being 'character,' and makes a human being a 'character' of one sort or another—to carry out this plan well, in this Installment 21, I need to return to meditating about the complicated nature of prudence, especially its constituent, or integral, parts,

In his *Summa theologiae* (2a2ae, qq. 47–53), St. Thomas Aquinas engages in a detailed study of the nature of prudence as a command and control virtue that integrates memory of past circumstances (hindsight) and understanding of present circumstances (insight) to develop foresightedness and keen-sightedness about how best to integrate use of all our psychological power to make healthy and safe choices in future circumstances.

Considered in this way, prudence is a complicated psychological habit of practical and productive understanding that integrates in the individual circumstance the habit of right reason (*recta ratio*, in

Latin) with the habits of true loving (*verum amandum*, in Latin) and choosing well (*bene eligens*, in Latin).

The prudent man is the well-counseled man who commands well in the here and now about the right choice to make about the means to an end in an individual, contingent, present or future, dangerous, and/or difficult circumstance, or situation. The subject about which the prudent man commands well is the singular contingent action—the right choice to make when surrounded by change and impending difficulty or danger.

Such a person must be skilled at *estimating*, guessing, well about the right choice(s) to make in difficult and dangerous, sometimes life-threatening, circumstances. To be able to do so, St. Thomas maintains that a person must possess the following 8 psychological parts of prudence: (1) a good memory; (2) insight, great induction skills; (3) teachableness (*docilitas*, in Latin); (4) quick-wittedness; (5) good practical and productive reasoning skills; (6) foresight; (7) circumspection, keen awareness of circumstances of an action; and (8) caution.

Since all the above 8 qualities chiefly focus on a person acting within circumstances, and since St. Thomas Aquinas claimed that 7 circumstances of a human act exist, the practical and productive virtue of prudence must be generated in its most perfect form by integrating the above 8 qualities with the following 7 acts of understanding: (1) who or what; (2) is doing what; (3) with what; (4) where; (5) why; (6) when; and (7) how (*Summa theologiae*, 1a2ae, q. 7, a. 3, respondeo).

Clearly, possessing all these qualities and being able simultaneously and successfully to integrate them within a dangerous and difficult situation is no easy task. Only a person with an extremely strong psychological character and in good physical health, surrounded by a lot of talented people and rich resources, can carry it off.

No wonder should exist, then, why prudence is rarely a dominant quality possessed by the young, and why most people tend to be victims, not masters, of their situation. Nor should any wonder exist why, to become a master of our circumstances, all of us need to become 'Brooklyn Existentialists,' 'Philosophical Paladins,' and 'Samurai Thomists.'

# Meditation Installment 22

*Some Unconventional and Colorful Friends I had During My Youth Who Helped Me Start to Form My Understanding of 'Brooklyn Existentialism' as Essentially a Species of Situationally Prudent Behavior*

In this Installment I will consider some 'a-normal' forms of colorful, situational behavior engaged in by a few friends I had during my youth that helped me start to form my initial understanding of 'Brooklyn Existentialism.' By 'a-normal' forms of behavior I mean ways of choosing to act in a problematic situation that I knew even early on were not the way most people would think of fixing a problem in a similar situation.

I have carefully chosen the word 'colorful' precisely because: (1) it is a quality, and (2) previously I have mentioned that, despite widespread human use of the word 'quality' to refer to a reality of some sort that modifies the behavior of acting subjects, for centuries, pseudo-intellectuals have reduced qualities to fictions and/or to physical quantities.

Consider, for example, how often we analogously use terms like 'warm,' 'hot,' 'cold,' 'sweet,' 'sour,' 'rough,' 'smooth,' 'bright,' 'dim,' 'lovely,' and so on to myriads of different things, actions, and behavior; and consider how accurately these terms communicate to us the nature of some action, person, or thing.

The above introductory points of clarification having been made, since I have already written about two such friends (Paul Ranieri and Vinny Palermo), I will start with Paul.

Returning to Paul, I have already mentioned how his general appearance and way of talking and walking immediately communicated 'mutual understanding' to others that he could be dangerous. Some more information about his background will help readers understand precisely why the whole of his being tended to communicate this reality.

Paul's uncle was the head of the Lucchese family in Connecticut, and his father was a 'Made Man,' who worked for one of the local 'families.' Among other things, as an adult, Paul became a bouncer in a strip club in Queens, New York, called 'Wiggles,' which Vinny Palermo had owned. He also worked for the Longshoremen's Union (ILA) in New Jersey and had collected dues for them.

These jobs had enabled Paul to acquire lots of money. He told me that, at one time, he had owned four houses worth over $1 million each and had had 4 mistresses living in 4 of these houses. While this claim might sound to many people like an exaggeration, knowing Paul, I took him at his word.

One day he told me what would sound to many people like an equally incredible story. He asked me whether I remembered Ernie Benedetto. I told him I had. (Ernie was hard to forget. He was a sociopath—a real nutcase).

Paul told me Ernie had been imprisoned because federal agents from a 3-letter agency had discovered Ernie had 'bunked' close to $1 million under floorboards in his attic ceiling. After Paul reported this to me, I checked online media to see whether I could find any news about the story, and I discovered that Ernie and his nephew had been arrested for processing millions of dollars worth of heroin. I immediately made the connection between what Paul had said to me and Gene Hackman's wild car chase through Bensonhurst under the elevated Brooklyn train line in the movie 'The French Connection.'

At the same time he had told me about Ernie, Paul told me he was annoyed with our friend Frankie Noviello (aka, 'Bullhead' and 'Apeman') because Frankie had told Paul he had hung up a picture of Paul's son in his jail cell. Incredulous and annoyed that Frankie had done this, Paul asked me, "What was he thinking? Why would he have done that?" I could think of no good answer to give to Paul.

Last, but not least, is a third report Paul had given me—about two of our friends 'Tomasulo' and sociopath John Burke.

Paul and I had known Tomasulo from hanging out with him at the PS 201 schoolyard a block from my house in Dyker Heights. We knew Burke from his being in our class in elementary school at St. Ephrem's.

Like many of our friends, many of us only knew each other and others in the neighborhood only by some nickname—like 'Charlie the Swede,' 'Butterass,' and so on. This is the way I had known Tomasulo.

To continue, Paul told me that Burke had been instrumental in getting Tomasulo three jobs—one in the US Air Force, the other in getting into the New York City Police Department, and the third was in becoming a Detective in the NYPD.

Aside from being an arrogant jerk and a sociopath, Burke was academically very smart and a brilliant mathematician. Since

Tomasulo wanted to get into the US Air Force and knew he could not pass the test to do so, he paid Burke to take the test for him.

Somehow, Burke was able to falsify identification and take the test for Tomasulo. Of course, Burke passed it with flying colors, and Tomasulo was elated by this outcome.

Shortly thereafter, however, Burke's high score on the test nearly got Tomasulo into trouble. Seeing how well 'Tomasulo' (Burke) had scored on the test, on several occasions, he was approached by a member of the Air Force to become an 'aeronautical engineer.' As a result, for the entire time he spent in the Air Force, Tomasulo had to lay low.

After he got out of the Air Force and wanted to join the NYPD, Tomasulo had paid Burke to take the test for him; and Tomasulo had no problem as a result. Nor did Tomasulo have a problem becoming a Detective in the NYPD. Paul told me that he drove Tomasulo to 1 Police Plaza in Manhattan, parked his car, and went upstairs with Tomasulo to get his Detective 'Shield,'—for which Tomasulo had paid $25,000 in cash.

Paul reported to me this was a stroke of good luck for Vinny Palermo because, several years after this, during the 1970s, Tomasulo was appointed to head the Police Department's Organized Crime Control Bureau (OCCB). Once he got into this position, Tomasulo got rid of Vinny's file from the Department's records!

While $25,000 might sound like an exorbitant amount to buy the Detective Shield decades ago, a reliable Bensonhurst friend of mine told me that, at the same time, Meade Esposito was 'nicely requesting' a $50,000 donation to the Democrat Party in Queens. Anyone who made that donation could subsequently run for a judgeship on the Democrat ticket and win hands down.

While some readers of this Installment might not approve of the 'a-normal' behavior of the youthful friends I describe above, crucial to note about it is how, in each case, the people involved in the scenarios reported above immediately induced the middle term of a practical and productive syllogism that enabled them to solve a problem confronting them; and, if they used any reasoning at all, they used a situational enthymeme—not an abstract logical syllogism—to resolve this problem.

# Meditation Installment 23

*How 'Augustinian-Sicilian, Political Prudence' is an Essential First Principle of the Colorful and Unconventional Behavior of 'Brooklyn Existentialist' Friends from My Youth*

Evident from the behavior of my friends Paul, Tomasulo, and Burke which I described in Installment 22 is that, in each instance in which they faced a situational problem: (1) they immediately sought to resolve the problem through harmonious team effort—actions that involved them applying in a single, cooperative, psychological operation the 8 integral parts of prudence and 7 circumstances of an act; and (2) they did so by implicitly conceiving of the nature of all political regimes in the way any psychologically healthy 'Augustinian-Sicilian' would do: 'All political regimes constituted by professional politicians in charge of their administration are essentially unjust: are large-scale, organized-crime gangs.'

By nature, all such political groups are essentially composed of flawed parts that, when harmoniously unified, generate a product that is somewhat psychopathic and operates like a psychopath. This is so because the essential organizational principles of these gangs do not have the common good of the citizens under their rule as their common good.

Their common good is to keep the administrators of the State in power. In such a professional political organization, the head bureaucrats who run it tend to think 'they are the organization—they are the State.' By long historical experience, commonsense Sicilians know these politicians tend to think this way. And so did anyone in my Dyker Heights, Bensonhurst, Bay Ridge neighborhood that was dominated by this form of Sicilian political prudence.

Of course, reacting consistently and with common sense against such politicians in contingent circumstances sometimes fails. When this happens, friends of mine like Paul immediately understood they had made a mistake and tried to learn from having done so.

For example, Paul knew he had made a serious mistake trying to maintain five houses with four mistresses, while simultaneously being married. I know this because one day his wife found out about this situation and sued him for divorce.

Somehow, she was able to win in court, and Paul had to go into bankruptcy to remain somewhat economically solvent. He wound up owning one small house, within walking distance of the Gateway National Park in Great Kills, Staten Island.

When he told me about his regret, I had the good fortune of teaching an Ethics class to a group of largely cynical and skeptical undergraduates at St. John's University. Almost all of them tended to doubt the existence of universal ethical principles.

Racking my brain to find one, I asked Paul whether he had learned anything from the trouble he had gotten himself into by cheating on his 'then-current wife,' while simultaneously supporting four mistresses. Without batting an eye, he immediately gave me the following precise gem of wisdom I had been searching for: "Never cheat on your mistress with your ex-wife's best girlfriend!"—a universal moral principle the soundness of which none of my students, nor I, could refute!

# Meditation Installment 23

Aside from his interesting take on some universal moral principles, I always found Paul to be exceptionally charitable. For example, he frequently made donations of clothes and food to people in need during holidays. When a heavy snowstorm would hit Staten Island, if he had the time, he would put a plow on the front of his truck and shovel driveways, at no charge. If I needed someone to help me move something, or to work on something, he would always be volunteer to help me. And, if he went to a movie theater and had 'pirated' a newly released film, he would bring a copy to my wife and me ASAP.

Furthermore, as far as I could tell, he did all these acts of kindness out of a genuine love for other people. He never appeared to be doing so as penance to assuage a guilty conscience.

Whatever the case, unlike many of our contemporaries—especially Enlightened, professional politicians—Paul had a conscience in touch with reality, under the direction of which, I am convinced, as best he could, he attempted to do good and avoid evil in the individual situation. So did Vinny.

In the next Installment, I will attempt to explain why I have no doubt that a main reason Paul and Vinny could act under the influence of a relatively healthy conscience is because, apart from the 'Augustinian-Sicilian political prudence' they both possessed, they were, and still are, convinced about the reality of the 'human soul.'

# Meditation Installment 24

*Paul Ranieri's and Vinny Palermo's Political 'Sicilian-Augustinianism' and Metaphysical and Moral 'Brooklyn Existentialism'*

To people who have not known them and are not familiar with the way 'Brooklyn Existentialists' tend to think, psychologically considered, from youth through adulthood, Vinny Palermo's and Paul Ranieri's behavior might reasonably appear to be largely irrational, ethically vicious, criminal, and lacking in common sense. On the contrary, having known both of them fairly well, I am certain such negative qualities do not accurately capture the psychological makeup of Vinny any more than they do that of my friend Paul, or the princes, kings, cardinals, and pontiffs of Christendom during the pejoratively named 'Middle Ages.'

About the Roman Catholic Church, Hilaire Belloc (one of the greatest uncommon commonsense authors of the 20th-century) once said somewhere: "The Catholic Church is an institution I am bound to hold divine—but for unbelievers, a proof of its divinity might be found in the fact that no merely human institution run with such knavish imbecility would have lasted a fortnight."

Unhappily, while what Belloc says above about the Catholic Church contains much truth, I would never describe Vinny's behavior or that of Paul as having been conducted with "knavish imbecility." Like all young and adult human beings, at times their behavior was imprudent. I suppose, some of Vinny's choices are still imprudent, periodically lack moral common sense. Nonetheless, neither one was mean, unscrupulous, or 'vicious' in the popular meaning of the term. Neither one behaved like a psychopath or sociopath.

While I did not know Vinny as well as I knew Paul, I first met both of them around the same time—when each of us was about halfway through elementary school. And I met Vinny through Paul.

As I mentioned in a prior Installment, I used to see Vinny a couple of times a week during the fall, winter, and spring at the PS 201 schoolyard. In the summer, I saw neither of them because I would be at our family summer cottage in Bertrand Island, Lake Hopatcong, New Jersey— where I also had several friends from Bayonne, New Jersey who were colorful characters and thought and behaved like 'Brooklyn Existentialists.'

Apart from meeting him at the schoolyard, pretty much every weekday after getting home from school, if I did not go to the schoolyard, I would go around the block to 81st St. between 10th and 11th Avenues to play stickball and other games with friends of mine—congregating around the front stoop of a classmate of mine from St. Ephrem's, Billy Ellis.

Pretty much every day I was there, I would run into Vinny because his girlfriend, Valerie (whose father was a 'Made Man') lived next to Billy. Whenever Vinny would visit Valerie, my friends and I would shoot the breeze with him for a while.

During my youth, I never found Paul or Vinny to be mean, unscrupulous, racists—to abuse children, the elderly; mistreat people they knew to be good, and so on. They tended to go out of their way to protect such people, and the communities in which they lived, from bullies and scoundrels.

In fact, I found them ethically superior to many clerics and mostly every professional politician I have ever met. If they ever lied, cheated, stole, gave someone a good beating, or worse, they did so to protect themselves and people who were their relatives, friends, and neighbors from some sort of abuse or danger.

In behaving this way within the context of what they rightly conceived to be the totalitarian, modern and contemporary, 'Enlightenment Sovereign State' (which considers itself, not God, to be the author and dispenser of all human rights and duties), Paul and Vinny were behaving like political 'Sicilian-Augustinians' and metaphysical and moral 'Philosophical Paladins' and 'Samurai Thomists': somewhat flawed, 'Brooklyn Existentialists.'

From the way I have described Paul and his behavior in previous Installments, no need exists for me to explain to my readers why I think these sobriquets fit him. Just why they fit Vinny I will attempt to explain in my next Installment.

# Meditation Installment 25

*'Brooklyn Existentialists' as Political, Metaphysical, and Moral Enigmas*

Toward the end of Installment 24, I referred to Paul Ranieri's and Vinny 'Ocean' Palermo's behavior as a conflation of political 'Sicilian-Augustinianism,' metaphysical and moral 'Philosophical Palladianism,' and 'Samurai Thomism'—that is, as 'Brooklyn Existentialism.' I did so because, at that time, I was considering meditating in Installment 25 about how the organizational psychology of Paul and Vinny was no aberration in the Dyker Heights, Bensonhurst, Bay Ridge neighborhood of my youth.

This psychological disposition ('Brooklyn Existentialism') heavily influenced the behavior of the majority of young people and adults who lived around where I was raised—from members of everyday, middle-class families to 'Families' of organizational community leaders like Joe Profaci, Joe Colombo, Carlo Gambino, and those they employed.

I mention this reality because, as I have already indicated in prior Installments, a main reason I am writing these missives is to help my readers develop a habit of psychological understanding that will enable them: (1) better to comprehend the present, dangerous, cultural and civilizational situation that surrounds all of us today; (2) keep themselves, their friends, and families as safe as really possible within it; and (3), as much as possible, flourish, and live as happily as possible by understanding this situation's nature. This understanding is 'Brooklyn Existentialism.'

Ever since I started my teaching career, I have always had as a chief goal to improve the intelligence of my students in the sense of communicating to them a habit of understanding that would enable them to live happier lives. Over the past several decades, I have been increasingly aware that the best way to do this is by getting beginning students to understand that they cannot become masters of their circumstances—become more highly and deeply educated— unless they first understand their current situation.

The human situation in which we all live for any length of time politically is a religious and cultural one. Only a people that accepts the reality of providence guiding their lives can develop and flourish politically. Such a people accepts as evident the reality of the moral virtue of prudence (in the form of individual and cultural and transgenerational common sense) and the metaphysical reality of the existence of a beneficent God, or Supernatural entity, and of a human soul. This includes self-declared, commonsense atheists.

A sign of the truth of what I have just said in the preceding paragraph is that all relatively sane adult human beings and children accept as evident: (1) that 'only human beings can be murdered' because only human beings possess 'a human soul'—not the soul of a plant or a brute animal); (2) that murderers can only be 'murderers' precisely because they violate the natural law commandment: 'Do not murder'; and (3) natural law is the Law of Providence that governs the behavior of all beings that inhabit the finite order.

For these reasons, none of the local 'organized crime leaders' in the neighborhood of my youth would tolerate any of their workers hurting innocent people. Nor would they do this themselves. In fact, 'Made Men' took an oath never to do so. Vinny 'Ocean' took this oath. For this reason, pretty much every media website that has information posted about him talks about the fact that he had a reputation of protecting children—those of other people, as well as his own.

Like Joe Colombo, Joseph Profaci, and Carlo Gambino, Vinny considered himself to be religious, a Catholic. Among other things, a 'Wikipedia' entry about him says he had: (1) been an altar boy; (2) attended Sacred Heart Church in Island Park, New York as a married adult; (3) took a personal interest in a trouble teenager named 'Richard'; (4) became Richard's 'godfather,' in the religious meaning of the term; and (5) allowed Richard "to stay at his home every weekend for a year, enabling the boy to study the Catholic sacraments in preparation for eventual Baptism, Communion, and Confirmation" (See: https://en.wikipedia.org/wiki/Vincent_Palermo).

At the same time, Vinny had taken an oath as a 'soldier' in the DeCavalcante 'family,' to protect innocent people from being hurt. Among other 'family' interests, to do so he was once ordered by someone in authority above him to execute the editor of the *Staten Island Advance* newspaper and criminal real estate developer Fred Weiss because Weiss was paying a caravan of New York City sanitation workers to use NYC sanitation trucks during hours from about 2 to 4 AM to dump dangerous medical waste on a site from which clean waste had been removed in Staten Island.

I was very familiar with this story, because, at this time, I was managing editor of a competing newspaper (the *Staten Island*

*Eagle*). Some Staten Island residents who had held a public meeting to publicize this problem told me some thugs had attended this meeting and had threatened them not to publicize what was going on. They also told me that the *Staten Island Advance* editor Fred Weiss had refused their request to write a story about what was happening. They asked me to publish it, and I did.

Shortly after I wrote the story, on 11 September 1989, Vinny and an 'associate' of his (Jimmy Gallo) drove to a condominium owned by Weiss's girlfriend. As Weiss was getting in his car after exiting the condominium, Vinny and Jimmy shot Weiss in the face.

Clearly, abstractly considered, Vinny's behavior appears to most morally healthy human beings that of a psychopath—unless one takes into consideration Vinny's 'Sicilian Augustinian' political background. Vinny was well aware that, far from New York City politics being an example of Ronald Reagan's and Puritan John Winthrop's 'Shining City on a Hill,' it was (and still is) a political cesspool run by some of the best politicians and judges money can buy.

Realizing that only a community protected by some military-like organization can hope to survive and protect its citizens against politically corrupt, ravenous wolves dressed in sheep's clothing, Vinny did what he considered to be his moral duty. Whether he was morally justified in behaving the way he did is not something I will attempt to judge at this point—or perhaps ever. For now, I simply consider it as one of the enigmas of being a 'Brooklyn Existentialist.'

# Meditation Installment 26

*Why Understanding the Enigma of 'Brooklyn Existentialists' Like Carlo Gambino and My Friend Nick is Crucial for Personal Well Being Today*

In prior Installments, I have emphasized the fact that, by natural inclination, all human beings with some common sense start every species of productive and profitable investigation with some understanding of their present situation. Such people naturally tend to reason from understanding where they have been, to understanding where they are, to understanding where they want to go.

In previous Installments, I have stressed that a main reason I am writing this personal and professional autobiography is as a guide to help readers of it live happier lives, and that 'living a happier life includes living a safer, more secure life.' Being able to do this, in turn, requires that we tend to understand the psychological make-up (the way they are disposed to think and choose) of people with whom we interact— whether on a frequent or infrequent basis. As Aristotle is well-known to have said more than two millennia ago, "As a person is disposed to think, so a person is disposed to choose."

More than understanding the psychological make-up of people with whom we interact, safely to flourish within the context of every human situation, a person needs to know precisely how 'respectfully' to talk to this or that person in the present situation.

To do so, as I have already mentioned, the psychological make-up of a 'Brooklyn Existentialist' always uses a conflation of the 8 integral parts of prudence and the 7 circumstances of an act. Three of these eight integral parts are easy to remember: hindsight (memory), insight (induction, or inductive understanding), and foresight (being able to anticipate the future). Together with the seven circumstances of an act, the other five integral parts of prudence—teachability, quick-wittedness, sound reasoning ability, circumspection, and caution—are psychological qualities that enable hindsight, insight, and foresight to be productively and profitably applied within individual circumstances.

In this Installment, as a sample of just such a productive and profitable discussion, I refer to a personal conversation Carlo Gambino had once initiated with a Bensonhurst friend of mine named Nick Purpura.

While I had not known Nick when we were both young, for more than 40 years he has been one of my closest friends with whom I have worked on many projects.

Nick is one of the greatest salesmen and most fearless and patriotic persons I have ever met. The only other individual I know who equals him in salesmanship, fearlessness, and patriotism is my young friend, James O'Keefe III—both of whom equal Donald Trump in these three traits.

During his youth, in addition to loaning money at rates higher than those charged by local banks and lending institutions, Nick used to sell guns to different 'Family' members. As an adult, after serving in the U.S. Special Forces in Alaska and then joining and serving in the U.S. Navy, Nick went on to sell weapon systems to the

Israelis as a General Partner and Managing Director of Bear Stearns Companies, Inc..

While at Bear Stearns, Nick was a money machine. At their high point, the Departments he oversaw were bringing in over 4% of the net worth of the Firm worldwide. (I know this for a fact because I saw written testimony to this percentage number given by Bear Stearns's attorneys during arbitration in which Nick was once engaged.) Nick was bringing in so much money to the Firm that he was asked to share his office with then-CEO/Managing Partner Alan Courtney ('Ace') Greenberg and the prior CEO/Managing Partner Salim' ('Cy') Lewis.

After he had retired from the military and had gone to work for Bear Stearns, Nick told me Carlo Gambino had met with him in Bensonhurst one day and had asked Nick whether Nick might be able to give him some inside information about investment opportunities.

Nick's 'respectful' reply to Mr. Gambino was that, unfortunately, Nick could not do so because: (1) he would never be disloyal to an employer, and behaving in this way would be an act of disloyalty to his employer; (2) giving Mr. Gambino such information would constitute 'insider trading'—a criminal offense; and (3), if law enforcement agencies ever learned of him engaging in this kind of activity and exposed him for so doing, he would bring shame to fellow Italians and would be publicly called 'a Guineau.'

Nick told me Mr. Gambino's response to what he had said was not to argue with, or threaten, him. It was to break out in a broad smile, gently tap him on his cheek, point his index finger at him and say, 'You are a good boy!'

Sometime shortly thereafter, on the day he was married and he went to his wedding reception, Nick was shocked to learn that, included within his wedding Package was a free 'Venetian Hour' paid for by Carlo Gambino!

I include this information in this Installment because, far from hating the truth and loving dishonesty, in my Dyker Heights, Bay Ridge, Bensonhurst neighborhood, like all psychologically healthy human beings 'Family leaders' like Carlo Gambino loved the truth, honesty; but they hated hypocrites—people who were not what they claimed to be.

They considered such people not to be 'Standup guys.' They were 'Rats'—undependable and unpredictable people who endangered the community because they could not be trusted. As a result, these leaders tended to treat people who behaved in this way with contempt—as those not among 'the innocents' who were never to be harmed.

Nick Purpura had (and still possesses) a masterful understanding of this 'Brooklyn Existentialist' psychological disposition. As result, he was not only able to survive in his community while disagreeing at times with its leaders. He was (and still is) able to do so safely, productively, and profitably. We can learn much from him about how to live in the same way in the perilous times in which we now live and the more dangerous ones we are likely to face in the not too distant future.

# Meditation Installment 27

*My Holy Saturday 2024 Lamentations with Dominic Profaci about the Contemporary Moral Decay of the United States and Dominic's Father's Unmatched Ability to Inculcate Common Sense Through Communicating Mutual Understanding (CMU)*

My 'Brooklyn Existentialist' friend Dominic Profaci phoned me this past Holy Saturday afternoon to apologize for not having returned my St. Patrick's Day 2024 phone greetings to him. Dominic and I have been exchanging phone calls on this day ever since his son-in-law, Pat Murphy, was killed in the World Trade Center bombing.

In remembrance of that day, if I have not already been in contact with him, Dominic usually phones me from an Irish pub as he raises a pint of Guinness and has a corned beef meal in memory of Patrick.

Dominic went on to tell me that he had been exceptionally busy and his conscience was bothering him for not having returned my phone call. What finally prompted him to do so, he reported, was his disgust at hearing on Good Friday that Joe Biden planned to issue a proclamation on Easter Sunday, 31 March 2024, declaring that date national 'Transgender Day of Visibility.'

As part of his lamentation, Dominic remarked how, like increasing numbers of Americans, Biden appeared to have no conscience, no moral compass, no sense of moral obligation or duty. My immediate reply to him was: "Where is Joe Profaci when we need him? Were he still alive New York City and the US would not have culturally declined the way it has. Talk about 'organized crime,' professional US politicians tend to be among the biggest gangsters there are."

Dominic wholeheartedly agreed with my reply. In addition, we both agreed that his father's uncommon, ethical common sense had enabled him repeatedly to understand precisely what move to make in the individual situation that would minimize the damaging, short- and long-term 'cultural rot' that people who lack moral common sense tend to have.

As we meditated about these topics, I immediately recalled a story my brother Jimmy had told me about an event that had happened at St. John's Prep in downtown Brooklyn one day during the early 1950s which required the prudent common sense of Dominic's father quickly and peacefully to resolve.

My brother Jimmy used to travel to the Prep on the same bus with Dominic's brother Sal and his cousin Iggy. As they exited the bus, Sal had accidentally bumped into a neighborhood teenage hoodlum named 'Cheech' (in no way related to my father's friend 'Cheech').

Cheech made the mistake of pushing Sal and threatening him with violence. Sal's immediate response was to hit Cheech in nose with his hardcover biology book—causing the nose to bleed.

Sal, Iggy, and my brother proceeded to walk into the school. As they did so, Cheech yelled out that he was going to get Sal after school. To protect himself, Sal phoned his father and told him what had happened.

In one of their classes, my brother Jimmy, Iggy, and Sal used to sit in the last row by the window. Sometime in the late morning or early afternoon, my brother saw Mr. Profaci's limousine pull up outside the front door of St. John's Prep and Mr. Profaci stroll inside.

My brother reported to me that, after they were dismissed from the School that day, nothing happened. Cheech never showed up. In fact, Jimmy never saw Cheech again while he attended the Prep. He did see Cheech outside the Prep several years later, however, when Jimmy stopped by the School one day.

This trouble with Cheech had occurred while the Korean War was then raging. When my brother saw him after graduating from the School, Cheech was dressed in a United States Army uniform.

Apparently, this incident involving Mr. Profaci's ability to communicate mutual understanding wound up becoming a life-changing teachable moment in the life of Cheech—from which he learned some much-needed humility and docility.

Either that, or some politically influential citizen and patriot had given Cheech's name to someone at the local draft board as a perfect candidate with just the right qualities that the U.S. Armed Forces needed to help win the conflict in Korea.

# Meditation Installment 28

*Brother Jerome 'Meric' Pessagno, CFX, and 'Tough Tony' Anastasia as Grand Masters of CMU Conversation*

As the title of this Installment indicates, it is a meditation on the uncommon, commonsense CMU conversational skills of two extraordinary individuals, from my Bay Ridge, Dyker Heights, Bensonhurst neighborhood: (1) My high school Latin teacher, saintly Brother Meric (Jerome 'Meric' Pessagno, CFX) and (2) 'Tough Tony' Anastasia (aka, 'Anastasio').

Aside from teaching Latin, Brother Meric was a brilliant linguist, orator, and coach of the Xaverian High School debating team. So successful was he as a debate coach that, while I was in attendance at the School, his debaters had won four successive national Catholic High School debating championships in Washington, D.C.

While he was a religious Brother, as a youth Meric had been surrounded by great wealth and privilege. For example, a relative of his (my recollection is that it was his uncle) had owned and operated the Circle Line Boat Tours around Manhattan.

In addition, in appearance, he looked, spoke, and carried himself like the actor Claude Rains. While his standard mode of dress at the School was the typical black religious habit and white collar, when he left the High School, he always covered this habit with a full-length black cape.

The story I am about to tell is about simple, one-way conversational excellence (which, for the situation, appeared to be two-way conversation). It was reported to me personally by Meric several decades after he had left teaching at Xaverian High School.

It does not relate to Meric's oratorical skills (which were magnificent). Instead, it treats of the masterful commonsense rhetorical skills of one of our local Italian-American community organizers—'Tough Tony' Anastasia.

While many readers of this Installment have likely 'heard' the names 'Tony' and 'Albert Anastasia' (aka, 'Anastasio') they might be unaware that the union boss 'Johnny Friendly' portrayed by actor Lee J. Cobb in the movie 'On the Waterfront' was based on Tony Anastasia—younger brother of Albert.

Of the two Anastasia brothers, Albert tended to be the more famous. As boss of 'Murder Inc.'—an enterprise reportedly responsible for around 400 to 1000 contract killings between 1929 and 1941—he was also the more feared and fearsome of the two.

Albert had a local reputation for having a mercurial temper, and he appears to me to have been somewhat sadistic, sociopathic. In short, he was lacking in that 'Brooklyn Existentialist' common sense about how to treat innocent people that many of our great community organizers, including Carlo Gambino, held dear.

As a result, during his tenure as head of 'Murder Inc.' and boss of the 'International Longshoremen's Association' Brooklyn waterfront (ca. 1945–1957), Albert had made a lot of enemies—including Mr. Gambino. As a result, apparently under the direction of Mr. Gambino, Albert met with an unfortunate 'accident,' which led to his death, on 25 October 1957 in the barbershop owned by my friend Nick's grandfather in the 'Park Central Hotel' in Manhattan.

Returning to Meric and his debating team, he was exceptionally proud of his debaters and wanted to reward them for all the great work they had done during their first three years. As part of this reward, he desired to take the team in style to Washington, D.C., for its last debating performance. To do this, he planned to have them driven to our national Capitol in a stretch limousine and housed while there in a penthouse suite at one of D.C.'s leading hotels.

To do that, economic common sense told him he needed money—which he estimated to come to a minimum of $2,000. To get the money, he decided to write to the presidents of the eight local banks in and near Bay Ridge, Brooklyn, at the time.

In the letter, he explained the reason for his requiring the money, and the fact that he thought their contributing to honoring the students in this way would be great local public relations on their part for which they would be publicly praised by Xaverian High School and eventually richly rewarded.

To his amazement, after waiting over two weeks, he had received not one reply from any of the bank presidents. Undeterred by this minor wrinkle in his plan, since Xaverian High School had many persuasive and influential personages whose sons were in attendance at the time, Meric spoke to one of them he had as a student in class—reported to me to be the son of Tony Anastasia.

Knowing that his father was head of the International Longshoreman's Association (ILA) at the Brooklyn waterfront, and that his Union collected dues from its member-ship, Meric asked Tony's son whether he would be willing to set up an appointment for him to talk to his father. Tony's son was happy to accommodate.

This being the case, several days later Brother Meric went to the Brooklyn waterfront early one morning to meet with Tony Anastasia in his office. After spending a few minutes in his waiting room, Meric said he was invited in and sat down across from the Union boss. Before relating to me the rest of the story, Meric told me the immediate sensation he had of meeting Tony was that of being in the presence of 'brute animal power.' He said the only experience he had ever had that approximated this was a prior interview he had conducted with Jimmy Hoffa.

Understanding his situation and 'respectfully' relaying the tale of the letters he had written to the bank presidents and the way that not even one had had the courtesy to reply to him, Meric told me Tony was totally dumbfounded by his report.

For several minutes—which had seemed much longer to Meric—he said Tony was so shocked by this 'act of disrespect and lack of common sense' that all he could do was shake his head back-and-forth to the left and right, while quietly muttering, *sotto voce*, "This is terrible, 'Bruddah.' This is terrible. After repeating this phrase three or four times, 'with all due respect,' Meric inquired of Tony what precisely he had meant when he said, "This is terrible."

Immediately, Tony responded to him like a no-nonsense, commonsense man on a commonsense mission who had immediately figured out precisely what was the problem and how immediately to resolve it.

In answer to his question, he told Meric: "Obviously, what happened here, 'Bruddah,' is that the bank presidents never got your letter. I'll tell you what I'll do. I will have my secretary phone each of these bank presidents right now while you are here, and I'll see whether we can straighten this problem out today.

And that is what Tony immediately did. A few minutes later, the first bank president phoned him, and Tony reported the problem to him. He said, "I have a 'Bruddah' Meric from Xaverian High School in Bay Ridge in my office. He tells me something terrible has happened. A couple of weeks ago, he wrote you a letter asking you to donate $4,000 to his debating society as a gesture of good public relations for which eventually you would be richly rewarded...."

As he was speaking, Meric tried politely to interrupt and correct what Tony was saying by holding up two fingers to indicate that the monetary figure was $2,000, not $4,000. Tony's body-language response was to shake his head back-and-forth, left to right while holding up four fingers.

He then continued, saying: "Obvious to me is that you never got the letter. I would like for us to resolve this problem now. So, would you please have someone from your office deliver $4,000 in cash to 'Bruddah' Meric by 4:00 PM today at Xaverian High School?"

Regarding the result of the meeting, Meric told me that, after leaving Tony's office and returning to the High School, at 4:00 PM on the dot, the School's doorbell started to ring. Thanks to the persuasive one-way talk posing as two-way conversation of Tony Anastasia, Meric received $32,000 (no small sum of money in those days) in cash in brown paper bags!

Recently I researched online the United States currency inflation rate since 1963—the year Meric's debating team had traveled to Washington, D.C. until now—toward the end of summer 2024. That inflation rate increase is 10%.

This means that, to take the same trip today that the Xaverian debating team took in 1963, if he wanted to receive the equivalent in the fall of 2024 to the $2,000.00 he had requested in 1963, were Meric alive today, he would have to ask for a minimum of $20,000 from each of the bank presidents ($160,000.00, in total)—with the hope that, at least one would reply positively.

This also means that, to fulfill Tony Anastasia's request in 2024, each bank president would have to have to deliver $40,000 a piece in brown paper bags to Xaverian High School by 4 PM on the day requested. This amount included Tony's *VIG* on the money—Tony doubling the donation to Brother Meric because of the discourteous way the bankers had treated his initial letter to them. This means that, at today's prevailing rate of inflation, Tony would be requiring these bankers to cough up $320,000 in cash—no small sum of money today!

While Tony's talk might have lacked some linguistic eloquence, it masterfully and succinctly contained and applied with highest intensity and economy the CMU form of one-way, commonsense speaking.

Concretely and precisely, it evinced Tony's comprehension of: (1) the nature of his audience and (2) the way to speak to his listeners 'nicely and respectfully' (as if engaging in a pleasant, two-way conversation with them). Any of them with 'Brooklyn Existentialist' common sense, however, clearly understood Tony was 'making them an offer they could not refuse.'

# Meditation Installment 29

*In its Moral Principles, is 'Brooklyn Existentialism' a Species of 'Situation Ethics' and/or 'Moral Relativism'?*

To anyone who has ever heard about and properly understood the nature of the ideologies (species of sophistry) commonly called "Situation Ethics' and/or 'Moral Relativism' the ethical principles of 'Brooklyn Existentialists' might appear to fit into one or both these categories.

'Situation ethics' is commonly said to teach that what makes individual human actions good or bad is not the act a person performs. It is the result of this act. In contrast, 'Moral Relativism' is commonly said to teach that no universal moral principles exist. Calling an individual act morally 'good' or 'bad' is identical to saying, "I like this, and I don't like that."

Both these ideologies are species of the sort of psychological crap, sophistry, that contemporary propaganda institutes masquerading as colleges and universities serve to unsuspecting students as part of the means they use to defraud them and/or their parents of their money.

As the commonsense Scottish philosopher Alasdair MacIntyre reported in his 1981 bestselling philosophical work *After Virtue* (Notre Dame, Ind.: University of Notre Dame Press), the entire language of contemporary moral discourse in academia is in disarray. Like the majority of courses taught in these misnamed 'higher educational institutions' worldwide today, nobody tends to know what he or she is talking about related to ethics/moral science.

In answer to the question about which I have indicated above I plan to meditate in this Installment, my answer is 'No!' In its moral principles, despite the way it might appear to some contemporaries, 'Brooklyn Existentialism' teaches nothing like 'Situation Ethics' or 'Moral Relativism.' The ethical/moral teaching of 'Brooklyn Existentialism' is simply a species of the natural law, organizational moral psychology of Aristotle as this was improved upon by the great, Italian Christian philosopher and theologian St. Thomas Aquinas.

Precisely what is this moral/ethical teaching is fairly easy to explain once a student has had his or her intellect scrubbed clean of all the misinformation about whatever he or she might have previously heard or read about the teachings of St. Thomas and of the nature of ethics/moral science. In my opinion, 99% of the academics who pride themselves in being students of St. Thomas Aquinas have no idea of pretty much any of his philosophical principles—including his moral/ethical principles—and the way he used them. Worse: they do not tend to know even what he meant by the term 'principle.'

During the 20th century, and first quarter of the 21st-century, such self-professed 'Thomists' have been largely responsible for the philosophical and theological 'knavish imbecility' and lack of administrative common sense that has come forth from 'leaders' of the Roman Catholic Church. Apart from some of my teachers, a few students of mine, and some professional colleagues of mine and their students whom I trust, I would caution students to consider such

'Thomists' intellectually suspect until proven competent beyond a shadow of a doubt.

In prior Installments, I have already presented readers of these meditations with an understanding of some of the philosophical principles St. Thomas Aquinas uses and the way he uses them. Chief among these is that *St. Thomas's philosophical teaching is essentially a trans-generational, cultural and individual, behavioral organizational psychology generated by the practical, productive, and contemplative virtue of prudence*!

Thomas teaches that philosophy is simply a traditional psychological habit embedded within a culture and an individual of applying the 7 integral parts of prudence and 8 circumstances of an act to understanding the nature and behavior of organizational wholes. This traditional habit includes understanding how to build, grow, maintain, dismantle, and destroy organizational wholes within individual situations. Thought about as such, 'properly speaking,' philosophy is essentially 'Situational Philosophizing'—concrete philosophizing within a situation.

Recall that, in past Installments, I have emphasized that: (1) 'Brooklyn Existentialism' understands 'philosophy' to be identical with 'science'; and (2) the chief interest of philosophy/science is to understand 'real organizational action'—how real organizations behave within some present time and place, in the here and now. Considered in this way, St. Thomas maintains that the situation/circumstances of an act enters into the specification of the act—including into the act of doing philosophy, or 'philosophizing.'

Talking in this way about the nature of philosophy and science 'properly speaking' and as 'classically understood' by leading Western philosophers like Aristotle and St. Thomas tends totally to befuddle contemporary Western 'philosophers' because they tend to be historical ignoramuses. It also tends to be totally incomprehensible to most contemporary college and university teachers of Aquinas's work because they tend to reduce his philosophizing to an abstract, systematic logic.

Nevertheless, that what I have described above is the actual teaching of Aquinas is easy to show. A popular idiomatic expression in the West is that, 'Circumstances alter cases.' For example, telling what Plato called a 'noble lie' to a person who is unaware that he or she has a terminal disease for the chief aim of sparing that individual severe emotional stress is specifically different from lying to a judge and the jury about the behavior of the person on trial for murder. This act of lying in court is commonly called 'obstruction of justice.' Nothing is noble about it.

Analogously, 'strictly speaking,' a person who is on the verge of starving to death who purportedly 'steals' food and water from someone who is a billionaire is no thief at all, steals nothing. By natural law of self-preservation, he or she is ethically entitled to the food and water.

While the claims I have just made above might fall on a deaf ear when heard by some sadist or psychopath like Albert Anastasia, they would be quite audible and commonsensical to his brother Tony.

Imagine what psychological stress Tony Anastasia must have had to endure for decades as a budding 'Brooklyn Existentialist' and younger brother of Albert! While this might be hard to do, 'Tough Tony' was clearly, in many ways, one of the good guys and a 'Brooklyn Existentialist.'

Were what I have just said not true, what Tony said to FBI agents after he had learned of his brother's 1957 execution in Manhattan would be incomprehensible: "I ate from the same table as Albert and came from the same womb, but I know he killed many people, and he deserved to die." (Reported in an August 1962, FBI memo; cited online on 20 September 1999; linked to as: *The Smoking Gun. Tough Love. New York*). Lucky for Tony that Albert was dead when Tony had said what he did. Otherwise, Albert would have considered him to be a 'rat' and would undoubtedly have put out a 'hit' on him.

Even luckier for Tony was that he died of a heart attack shortly after he reportedly had secret meetings with FBI agents in which he: (1) told agents "about a variety of Mafia matters, including which gangsters were allied with Teamsters boss Jimmy Hoffa"; (2) had requested that the information he had given to them "be disseminated only to FBI agents and Attorney General Robert F. Kennedy"; and (3) had said he did not want U.S. attorneys to know of his cooperation because he "felt that this was a politician's job and continually changing." (Cited online on 20 September 1999; linked to as: *The Smoking Gun. Tough Love. New York*).

In other words, having the uncommon commonsense of a 'Brooklyn Existentialist' philosopher, Tony had enough 'street smarts' to suspect he could trust the agents with whom he had met and Robert F. Kennedy not to 'sell him out' about what he had told them. At the same time, he had bought enough influence with U.S.

attorneys over the years (especially in New York) that he would have to have been a moron to trust them not to sell him out. A moron he was not.

No wonder that the body of 'Tough Tony' Anastasia is interred in sacred ground in Holy Cross Cemetery, Brooklyn, but the body of his brother Albert was refused entry there. In many ways, I suspect Mr. Gambino would have told Tony the same thing he said to my friend Nick, "You are a good boy!"

Good reason exists that he would have, including that, after Albert died, Mr. Gambino allowed Tony to stay on as boss of the Brooklyn waterfront until Albert died of heart failure in Long Island College Hospital on 01 March 1963. Agreeing with Tony that Albert 'deserved to die,' Carlo Gambino was not so gracious to Albert. Commonly accepted in Dyker Heights and Bensonhurst at the time was that Mr. Gambino was one of the 'Brooklyn Existentialist' bosses who had voted for Albert to face his Creator and receive his 'Divine Reward.'

# Meditation Installment 30

*Recovering a Commonsense Understanding of Ethics/Moral Science and Metaphysics as Species of 'Prudent Situational Philosophizing' (PSP)*

In previous Installments, I have noted that Aristotle and St. Thomas Aquinas had conceived of, and practiced, philosophy as a species of individual and cultural behavioral psychology. They had consciously done so historically and 'scholastically' as members of a school—that is, of an institutional, educational team enterprise engaged in trans-generationally transmitting an improved, more precise, individual and cultural habit of understanding about the nature and behavior of changing organizational wholes within changing individual circumstances.

Considered as such (for example, in part, as creating and sustaining schools of higher learning, like colleges and universities that have lasted for centuries), practicing philosophy in this way is an awesome cultural task. Such a work essentially involves a majority of the adolescent and adult population within a culture freely cooperating to transmit from one generation to the next a habit of philosophizing as a species of wisdom (metaphysics) and prudence (ethics)—or uncommon common sense.

As Étienne Gilson and C. S. Lewis had understood, this kind of work simultaneously involves a prior generation passing onto a subsequent one the common understanding that man is a 'rational animal'—in the sense of being a prudent animal: an animal with a soul possessed of natural faculties of intellect, will, and passions/emotions capable of generating common and uncommon common sense.

Such an animal is a free agent that conceives of itself as having a moral/ethical duty and responsibility essentially related to its own health, safety, and happiness—and that of its species and future generations of human beings—to understand the nature and behavior of things: organizational wholes that surround it.

Intentionally doing so essentially involves, at a minimum: (1) individually, culturally, and institutionally inculcating within a present generation the habit of psychologically synthesizing the 7 integral parts of prudence and the 8 circumstances of an act for the chief aim of understanding the behavior of qualitatively different organizations within radically different situations; and (2) institutionally transmitting this habit to future generations.

Several centuries ago, Cartesian and Enlightenment 'philosophies' (falsely so-called) engaged in the reckless adventure of removing the human soul (and with it philosophy/science, metaphysics, common sense, and ethics 'properly understood') from the human body.

In the case of Descartes and his followers, they replaced the human soul with a 'nominalistic collection of clear and distinct ideas' to which they arbitrarily gave the name 'spirit'—which, in some inexplicable way, 'felt itself' to be related to a machine they conceptually identified as a body.

In the case of Rousseau, Kant, and Hegel, they replaced the human soul with a utopian-socialist and ideologically progressivist heap of 'Enlightened emotions' masquerading as the Spirit of Human History: (1) transcending all prior, scientifically un-Enlightened and ethically backward heaps of blind 'feelings'; and (2) for the first time causing 'Conscience' and 'True Science' to enter 'Human History.'

These asinine, Cartesian and Enlightenment 'fairytales' posing as real philosophy destroyed the centuries-old Western understanding of man as a 'rational animal.' In so doing, they threw into individual and cultural disarray a proper understanding of philosophy, science, ethics, metaphysics, and Western and global education. They could not help but do so because they essentially removed from Western education and future generations their rightful cultural inheritance of millennia of prior wisdom, prudence, and common sense.

Reversing the disastrous cultural and civilizational effects of such academic propaganda and stupidity is no easy job. I have been working on doing so most of my adult life. In fact, in 4 monographs I list below, within the past nine years, I think I have made significant progress in: (1) explaining, in a fairly commonsensical way, to most halfway intelligent adolescents and adults St. Thomas Aquinas's understanding of ethics/moral science and metaphysics as species of behavioral organizational psychology; and (2) in the process, identifying and explaining some essential principles of ethics/moral science and metaphysics Thomas repeatedly uses and how he uses them in both metaphysics and ethics/moral science.

In order to reach the most widespread audience I can, in these autobiographical Installments, I am reworking much of this prior work and presenting it in a more entertaining way as species of 'Brooklyn Existentialism.' By simplifying my understanding of St. Thomas's teaching in this way, I hope to give it more widespread, popular appeal so that it might provide much benefit and comfort to a maximum number of people in generations of readers to come.

For those interested in getting the maximum benefit out of these Installments, I suggest you read these recently published books of mine:

1) *A Not-So-Elementary Christian Metaphysics: Written in the Hope of Ending the Centuries-old Separation between Philosophy and Science and Science and Wisdom. Volume 1– Re-establishing an Initial Union among Philosophy, Science, and Wisdom: How Philosophy, Science, Is, and Always Has Been Chiefly a Study of the Problem of the One and the Many* (St. Louis, MO.: En Route Books & Media, 2015).
2) *Op. cit.: Volume 2: An Introduction to Ragamuffin Thomism* (St. Louis, MO.: En Route Books & Media: 2016).
3) *The Moral Psychology of St. Thomas Aquinas: An Introduction to Ragamuffin Ethics* (St. Louis, MO.: En Route Books & Media, 2017).
4) *How to Listen and How to Speak: Standing on the Shoulders of Giants to Renew Commonsense and Uncommonsense Wisdom in the Contemporary World* (St. Louis, Mo.: En Route Books & Media, 2021).

# Meditation Installment 31

*An Introductory Reflection about First Principles of Ethics and Morality 'Properly and not Properly Understood'*

Evident is that we cannot learn what we already understand. Nor can we learn if we misunderstand something and refuse to admit this is the case. As I learned decades ago, we always begin learning from our present psychological situation related to first principles.

For this reason, for more years than I can remember, during my first few days of classroom or online teaching, I would make sure to remove students' common misunderstandings of first principles of a subject before attempting to inculcate the 'proper understanding' of the nature of the subject. As Aristotle reminded us millennia ago, small mistakes about first principles in the beginning of an investigation tend to increase many times over as the research continues.

Regarding the nature of ethics/morality, the chief aim of a college or university course in ethics or moral activity as a first principle or starting point that spurs on investigation is not to introduce students to the language of moral discourse. Nor is it to teach students that ethics, morality, or moral activity/science exists.

As Aristotle and St. Thomas Aquinas understood centuries ago, the existence of ethics, morality, moral science is an evident first principle to any psychologically healthy child or adult from the readily-observable fact that, within all social communities, we human beings incline publicly to praise and blame, reward and punish human beings for choices we make.

According to them, we do so because we immediately induce as a first principle of ethics, moral science, that such acts of behavioral encouragement and discouragement are exercised as an external sign to members of a community—human beings naturally and universally incline to take for granted that some forms of human behavior are socially acceptable, and others are not. This external sign is an indicator (first principle) that, by nature, human beings possess internal human faculties of voluntariness as other first principles of ethical/moral activity.

*These faculties*, not principles of language or logic, *are chief first principles of ethics, morality, moral science*. And this is the case because these faculties are signs that, by natural endowment, human beings are inclined to be, and behave as, prudent animals.

We are animals naturally possessed of psychological faculties of intellect, will, and emotions/passions that enable us to execute 'freely chosen action': 'free choice,' 'free decision-making'; and we are naturally inclined to do so as perfectly as humanly possible under the direction of the moral virtue of prudence. (St. Thomas Aquinas, *Commentary on the Nicomachean Ethics of Aristotle*, Bk. 3, Lesson. 1, nn. 382–391.)

The reason we naturally seek to do so is easy to understand. A perfectly free agent is no fool. 'Strictly speaking,' fools are not free agents. They are not masters of their situation. They are mastered by it. They are slaves.

Note that a common mistake predominantly made by contemporary human beings (including most teachers of the ethics of Aristotle and Aquinas) is about first principles that tends to conflate 'being ethical,' 'moral,' with being 'ethically or morally right, or virtuous.' Aristotle and Aquinas did not make that mistake. Nor do I.

They did not 'chiefly' refer to ethical, moral, action as ethically, morally, right, or virtuous, action. They understood ethical, moral, action to be freely chosen action.

And they did not conflate freely chosen action with voluntary action. For them, an action can be voluntary without being freely chosen, but a freely chosen action is always voluntary. To be freely chosen, an action must be voluntary and 'premeditated'—deliberate, planned, intended, self-commanded.

The Greek etymology of the term 'ethics' and the Latin etymology of the words 'moral(s),' 'mores,' and 'morality' support the claims I have made in the preceding three paragraphs.

When used with a short letter 'e,' the Greek term for 'ethics' (*ethos*) refers to a habit. When used with a long 'e,' it signifies a custom. When talking about the *ethos* of a person in his *Rhetoric* (1377b), Aristotle referred to the word as meaning whether a person could be considered trustworthy, credible. Having *ethos* did not guarantee a person to be ethically virtuous.

When translated into Latin, the English word 'moral' is signified by the Latin singular case *mos*. The Latin word *mores* is the foundation for the English terms 'mores,' 'moral(s).'

This return to recalling the nature of first principles having been completed, in the next Installment I can start to go into more detail about the specific difference between voluntary action and freely-chosen action.

# Meditation Installment 32

*Voluntary, Freely Chosen, and Moral Activities 'Properly Understood' as 'Complicated Psychosomatic Practical Judgments'*

Talking about voluntary, freely chosen, and moral acts (or activities) as 'complicated psychosomatic practical judgments' might strike many readers as odd. Nevertheless, 'precisely and properly speaking,' this is what these acts are.

A main reason I make this point at the beginning of this Installment is because failure to do so is a chief reason we often have difficulty precisely distinguishing among these 'principles of human action' in general, and specifically as they relate to the teachings of St. Thomas Aquinas.

Apart from these problems, another difficulty related to understanding what St. Thomas teaches about these principles is complicated by the fact that—unlike Aquinas—most of us (including most teachers of the work of St. Thomas) mistakenly maintain that human beings possess a psychological faculty they commonly call 'free will.'

Dealing with this second misunderstanding first, St. Thomas maintains that human beings have a way of judging and an acquired habit that, in Latin, he called *liberum arbitrium*—'free choice'; but, 'strictly speaking,' we have no natural faculty or power (like the natural powers of sight or understanding) called 'free will.'

According to him, the human will is naturally determined in conjunction with the human intellect to pursue the human good—

human happiness as perfect human operation: a life of perfect human virtue.

In addition, just as a human being senses with his or her intellect and intellectualizes with his or her senses, when we exercise 'free choice,' we do so as a psychosomatic whole. We choose as one whole person—with a relatively healthy or sick personal soul and individually strong or weak psychological and physical powers of intellect, will, senses, emotions engaged in making what St. Thomas calls a 'judgment of choosing' (*iudicium de exigendis*, in Latin), 'appetitive understanding' (*intellectus appetitivus*, in Latin), and 'appetitive inquisitiveness *(appetitus inquisitivus*, in Latin).

For example, when we choose, we often do so in good health, or with a headache, feeling physically sick or psychologically guilty/ill—taking pleasure in the choice we have made or feeling guilty as Hell for deciding not to do what a healthy conscience told us to do (*Summa theologiae*, 1a2ae, q.14, a.1 and a. 2, and q. 83).

Freely choosing is not identical with a simple act of 'taking.' Indeed, even a simple act of taking is not so simple—anymore than is a simple act of 'hitting.' In fact, both these seemingly simple acts are acts of exercising judgment—putting acts of judgment into practice.

According to Aquinas, prior to making a choice, a person must engage in three distinct acts of 'intending' (or 'planning'), 'deliberating' (or 'counsel'), and 'consenting'—none of which a brute animal can perform. All require an individual person to compare and contrast acts being judged by an abstract (qualitatively higher and general) and concrete (qualitatively lower and specific) faculty of understanding about situational contingencies relative to personal strengths and weaknesses.

As I noted in a prior Installment, Thomas calls this qualitatively, lower faculty of understanding 'cogitative' or 'particular' reason. He refers to the higher faculty as 'universal' reason.

Since brute animals lack: (1) this power, (2) the 8 commonsense and integral properties of prudence this power generates, and (3) an ability to consider in conjunction with these properties the 7 circumstantial conditions in which an act occurs (the situation of an act), brute animals cannot: intend a choice; deliberate about the means to execute it; consent to choose it; or be or feel happy or sad the way human beings do for being morally virtuous or vicious.

In the next Installment, I will meditate more about the complicated nature of voluntary activity as a way of judging related generally and specifically to moral activity.

# Meditation Installment 33

*Why Accurately Judging Voluntary and Involuntary Moral Behavior is a Skill Crucial for Every Organizational Leader to Possess*

St. Thomas Aquinas starts his examination of Book 3 of Aristotle's *Nicomachean Ethics* by: (1) noting that, because moral virtue works by means of free choice, Aristotle defines it as a habit of right choice; (2) stating that Aristotle discusses free choice together with voluntary activity and willing; and (3) claiming that voluntariness is common to free choice, willing, and anything freely done. This is so because choice mainly considers means related to an end, and willing chiefly considers the end to which means relate.

Shortly after making these observations, St. Thomas says Aristotle's prior discussion of moral virtue indicates that, in matters of actions and passions that concern ethics: (1) anyone acting virtuously deserves praise; (2) anyone acting viciously deserves blame; (3) no praise is morally due to anyone for involuntarily performing virtuous acts; (4) no blame, but pardon, is morally due to a person who involuntarily performs vicious acts; and (5) sometimes Aristotle says that a person who involuntarily performs a vicious act deserves more than pardon—namely, pity.

According to St. Thomas, the reason for this is that pity is an emotional reaction that consists in feeling sad for someone. In contrast, pardon is a judgment of right reason (prudence) that involves lessening, or totally canceling, punishment and blame.

This distinction causes St. Thomas immediately to note that, because morally virtuous acts merit (1) rewards of praise and other goods and (2) morally vicious acts merit blame and other forms of punishment, Aristotle maintains that prudent legislators should find especially useful the study of voluntary and involuntary acts. Doing so will enable them to embody in legislation honors and rewards that will encourage citizens to be law-abiding and punishments to discourage them from being law-breakers.

Readers should note that engaging in such a study is not restricted to legislators. It is a crucial form of research into first principles of organizational behavior that anyone who expects to be a good or great organizational leader must master early on to avoid making a multitude of organizational mistakes later on.

According to Aquinas, Aristotle had maintained everyone who wants to study moral virtue and vice needs to study voluntary acts. And they need to do so at first externally—from the effects of these acts: the external signs of praise and blame, reward and punishment that their actions and choices first publicly receive!

Regarding the nature of first principles of understanding as first principles of right reason (prudential judgment), these immediately preceding statements of St. Thomas are vital for any prospective organizational leader and student of Aquinas to understand. They indicate that, throughout his *Nicomachean Ethics*, Aristotle repeatedly starts his method of investigation into first principles with negative induction and reasoning.

And this is the case whether these principles be: (1) those of concrete, practical and productive 'life experience' habits of induction and understanding which, in Latin, St. Thomas calls (*per aliud notum*—that is, 'known through means of another'—'known through practical or productive experience at living'); or (2) 'abstract, immediate, conceptual induction or under-standing known through itself'—that is, *per se* or 'self-evident' induction/understanding.

Every investigation into first principles must begin negatively, by way of what St. Thomas, in Latin, calls *remotio* (the way of 'remotion,' or 'removal') and *demonstratio quia* ('demonstration that' or 'demonstration from effect to cause')—from external signs to internal causes capable of generating those signs.

This negative way of proceeding must be used with respect to evidently known practical and productive principles (*per aliud notum* principles) because, for us to know them, we must immediately and intellectually induce, understand, what we externally sense to be an effect—external sign—pointing to an internal cause.

That this negative way of proceeding is evident with respect to 'conceptually abstract,' *per se notum* principles is due to the fact that we can only develop our ability to engage in this kind of 'abstract, conceptual' induction and understanding after many, 'really doable, concrete, judgmental acts' of practical and productive induction and understanding.

Hopefully, by this point, realizing this evident fact is a really doable deed for all the readers of this Installment.

# Meditation Installment 34

*Further Meditation about Why Every Investigation into First Principles Must Start Negatively and Some Astounding Implications of This Fact*

In Installment 33, from the standpoint of the natural order in which all human beings first learn, I indicated we do so by proceeding from what we first externally sense as external signs we observe in the behavior of some acting subject(s) essentially related to the internal causes of those signs. However, a much simpler way exists to explain the reality of this fact.

I explain this at the start of this Installment in case some reader(s) might still have some difficulty completely comprehending why this negative method is the only procedure human beings can follow to induce, understand, first principles: The nature of a first principle demands we use this procedure psychologically to apprehend it!

By nature, a principle is a starting point. A point is an 'in-divisible.' Considered as such, a point is a unity, 'a one.' All human beings in touch with reality form the concept of unity negatively—by 'denying,' 'negating,' divisibility as a quality present in some single body that is one, or has unity. For example, someone senses that a physical line has been cut. Prior to being cut, one line (one linear body) had existed. After being cut, two lines exist (two linear bodies existed).

This example indicates that all human beings form the identical concept of a real number (the number '2') by 'the action' of dividing a previously un-divided/not divided subject of sense awareness. A real number is not an abstraction or arbitrary psychological invention. Nor is it identical with a 'multitude,' or a 'plurality.' A plurality, multitude, is a 'heap,' 'stuff.'

As Aristotle rightly understood, a real number is a 'limited, or measured, plurality,' a 'limited, or measured, multitude.' For this reason, he had maintained that the first number is '2,' and that a unity, 'a one,' is not a real number.

Unity, being one, is the 'principle' of real number. In addition, he had stated that a measure must be homogeneous with the thing measured. Hence, we use one horse to measure, count, a number of horses (*Metaphysics*, Bk. 4, 120b19-20, Bk. 6, 1080a15-37, and Bk. 10).

Recall from a prior Installment that, toward the start of Part 1 of his *Summa theologiae* (1a, q. 1, a. 2), St. Thomas Aquinas had maintained that the whole of a science is contained in its principles. Since this is so, following Aristotle, he had claimed that philosophers, scientists, must begin their investigations by 'defining' their subject (genus or organizational whole) and the way that subject is studied. In other words, the whole of the science is virtually contained and its definitions.

To define their subject, philosophers, scientists, cannot simply pull out of the thin air some arbitrary or abstract, universal concept of what is their subject and the method (psychological habit(s)) they use to study it. The natural order of learning is first to observe the actions of subjects belonging to the same genus (organizational whole) and to define those subjects in terms of judging their behavior as 'concrete universals' and signs of internal faculties, powers/abilities, capable of causing them.

For example, someone who wishes biologically to study the behavior of cats must start by observing the real, universally concrete, behavior of cats—not by attributing to cats the behavior of horses or some abstraction. No competent biologist would do otherwise. We first measure (define) cats by the real, situational, behavior of cats—not by the real actions of horses or abstractions.

The implications of what I have just stated in the above two paragraphs for properly understanding the nature of philosophy, science, as a psychological human habit is nothing short of astounding. We do not first derive our understanding of definitions as abstract universals derived by logicians. We first derive them from commonsense observation made by commonsense individuals working as prudent organizational psychologists.

In the next Installment, I will consider some other astounding implications that follow from those same paragraphs related to understanding all species of virtue and the nature of organizational leadership.

# Meditation Installment 35

*Some Astounding Implications that Intellectually Follow from the Fact that 'Unity is the Measure of All Things'—and their Crucial Importance for the Contemporary World*

Well-known to anyone who has studied the teachings of Ancient Greek philosophers is that Protagoras of Abdera (485–415 B.C.) had maintained that 'Man is the measure of all things.' In contrast to Protagoras, equally well-known is that Aristotle had asserted 'unity is the measure of all things' (*Metaphysics*, 1053a).

Similarly well-known to students of St. Thomas Aquinas is his claim that 'being' (*ens*, in Latin) 'is what first falls into apprehension of the human intellect' (*Summa theologiae*, 1a, q. 12, a. 1, ad 3). This, however, does not mean Aquinas had thought 'being' (an existing thing or substance) could be understood apart from unity.

What first falls into the human intellect 'as comprehensible' is not some abstract concept, essence, substance, or genus called 'being.' According to Aquinas, a being (something) as "understandable,' 'intelligible' to a human intellect is 'limited' or 'measured' being—being as an 'indivisible intelligible' (what he referred to in Latin by the awkward term *indivisibilis intelligibilis*). Hence, what a child first intellectually knows is 'some existing action' apprehended as a moving unit, principle, or cause—not as 'Mommy' or 'Daddy.'

A main reason for this is because, as St. Thomas states, the essence of unity is to be a principle, cause, of order in the action, behavior, of some organized whole. According to him, Aristotle did not conceive of a unit, or unity, as some static way of being. Odd as it might first seem to us, Aristotle had claimed that the essence of unity consists in being a proximate cause and principle of order within the actions of an organized, real, generic, specific, or individual whole.

*As first conceived by the human intellect, unity is a quality* (an intrinsic principle, measure, limit) of how *qualitatively* great, perfect something is in 'the magnitude of its power and influence'—in its ability to cause order and organizational actions/effects widely and deeply in this material world in which we live.

The first experience every human being has of unity is of a 'resistance to internal division,' a 'unity of order,' or 'ordered unity.' The reason for this is that the only way a plurality can exist as a unity is by having a unity of order (a unity resisting internal division). And a unity of order can only exist within an organizational whole.

According to St. Thomas, Aristotle had maintained that we: (1) first name things according to the way we first understand their actions; and (2) first understand the actions of things through the way we best sense them. Since physical motion is the action best known by us as most evident to our senses, we first apply the term 'action' to some continuous (undivided) physical motion—a motion that gets its ordered unity from an *unbroken*, physical continuum in which it exists (*Commentary on the Metaphysics of Aristotle*, Lesson 3, n. 1805).

Not only do we first know real being in terms of continuous, rightly ordered action, according to Aristotle and Aquinas, continuous rightly ordered action is the goal of all philosophy, science. For this reason, St. Thomas says teachers of science tend to think they have finally achieved their goals as educators when they observe students they have taught artfully performing these activities in public. *A real philosopher, scientist, does not consider his or her habit of philosophy to be complete until it is exercised in act* (*Commentary on the Metaphysics of Aristotle*, Lesson 8, nns. 1860–1861).

As St. Thomas, following Aristotle, states in Book 1, Chapter 1 of his *Summa contra gentiles*, the 'office' (duty, moral responsibility) of a wise man consists in more than ordering and organizing things rightly. It consists in: (1) teaching others how to do likewise; (2) publicly refuting the errors of those who oppose truth; and (3) excluding such mistakes from becoming widespread within individual and cultural life.

Aristotle and Aquinas had spent decades of their lives doing intensely hard work to pass on to posterity an understanding of science, philosophy, as an individual and cultural behavioral psychology that could keep future generations wise and free. Sadly, immersed in a 'woke barbarism' that reduces the whole of wisdom, science, and philosophy to 'diversity,' 'pluralism,' and 'inclusion,' much of the contemporary world is starting to reap the impoverishing fruits and chains of the slavery of their own 'woke foolishness.'

My hope is that the uncommon commonsense principles of Aristotle and St. Thomas I am passing onto readers of these Installments will help protect them against experiencing these rapidly increasing evils.

# Meditation Installment 36

*Removing Some More Contemporary Misunderstandings regarding Aquinas's Teachings about the Nature of Philosophy/Science*

Because the contemporary West and world no longer share a common understanding of philosophy, science, I am convinced the best hope to escape from ever-increasing, daily, global madness and brutishness is through a world-wide recovery of the classical Greek understanding of philosophy/science. This understanding conceived of philosophy/science as a complicated individual and social psychology essentially caused by 'rational animals.'

Such animals have souls that contain faculties, powers, that can cause acts of common sense, prudence, and wisdom. These actions qualitatively transcend in psychological perfection acts of imagination, memory, emotion, and instinct that the psychological faculties of brute animals are capable of causing.

I am also convinced that: (1) our best hope of making such a recovery resides in globally spreading the actual teachings of St. Thomas Aquinas about the nature of philosophy/science; and (2) one of the biggest obstacles to doing this consists in avoiding the many, gross misunderstandings of what Aquinas actually taught about the nature of philosophy/science since he was buried in 1274.

In prior Installments, I already talked about some of these misunderstandings—including the widespread mistake of reducing his understanding of philosophy/science to an abstract, systematic logic. In this Installment 36, I want to focus attention mainly on what he actually says about the nature of philosophy/science in his magisterial *Commentary on the Metaphysics of Aristotle*. Doing so should make easily evident to readers how radically innovative and advanced were his and Aristotle's teachings about philosophy and science when contrasted to the 'taffy-pull' mess that globally masquerades as philosophy and science today.

Beginning in the first paragraph of his 'Prologue' to the abovementioned work, St. Thomas makes a radical, commonsense claim that no contemporary, Enlightened philosopher or scientist would likely think of making today: 'All arts and sciences share a single, main goal—to bring human beings to perfection by causing human happiness in us.' Eureka! What a novel idea! The chief goal of science is to make us happy, perfectly human.

As if this were not strange enough, within the same 'Prologue,' Aquinas maintains that the chief aim of a science is to investigate the 'proper,' or 'proximate' principles (causes) and 'properties' of a real genus.

Well-known to anyone who has investigated to any extent the history of Western philosophy is that philosophy, science, did not begin among the ancient Greeks with the study of the proximate principles, causes, of logic. It began with physics—wondering about principles, causes, of action (in the sense of 'motion').

As additional proof of this claim, I cite what St. Thomas says in Book 9, Lesson 3, n. 1805, in which he explains that, etymologically, words, names, are signs referring to actions we first understand. What children first understand is what they sensibly perceive. Since motion is what is best known to our senses, the Ancient Greeks first used the word 'actual' to refer to motion. After doing this, they extended the meaning of action more widely to any species of action whatsoever.

The most widespread mistake I have seen related to understanding the philosophical/scientific teachings of St. Thomas involves misunderstanding the subject, or genus, a logician considers to be identical with the subject, or genus, a philosopher/scientist studies.

As Aquinas correctly understood, in his logical work entitled the *Categories*, Aristotle speaks from the viewpoint of a logician, not from the viewpoint of a philosopher. The chief subject (genus) the logician investigates are the principles, causes, that transform abstract concepts into intelligible judgments and intelligible speech—the way human beings 'vocally express' signs, definitions, terms, words, names, that had been abstract, intelligible mental beings (essences, 'quiddities') into forms of intelligible speech.

In addition, according to him, as a logician understands it, the word 'substance' signifies ('means') the main subject of definition. For example, if I say that Socrates was a leading, ancient Greek philosopher, the main subject I am defining (specifying the meaning of) is 'Socrates'—not 'leading,' 'ancient,' 'Greek,' or 'philosopher.'

In contrast, by 'substance,' the main subject the philosopher, scientist, is specifying, defining, is the proximate cause of any action whatsoever—not a principle, cause, of intelligible speech. According to Aquinas, human perfection consists in possessing scientific understanding about every action and everything. (*Commentary on the Metaphysics of Aristotle*, Lesson 1, n. 9). Such understanding consists in knowing the proximate principles, causes, 'truth' about every action and everything.

Hence, St. Thomas concludes Book 1, Chapter 1, nns. 2–3 of his *Summa contra gentiles*, by stating: (1) truth has to be the ultimate aim of the entire universe; (2) the 'office,' 'duty,' of the same science is to defend the truth of one opposite and refute errors opposed to this truth; (3) the chief aim of someone who is wise must be to meditate especially about a first principle and refute mistakes opposed to it.

In the next Installment, I plan to say more about St. Thomas's teachings about philosophy, science, opposites, and substance.

# Meditation Installment 37

*Additional Meditation about St. Thomas's Teachings Related to Philosophy, Science, Contrary Opposites, and Substance*

Well-known to avid sports fans is that, when a player or team is in a 'slump,' the player, coach and manager instinctively tend to attend to solve the problem by having the player or team returned to practicing 'the basics.' By 'the basics' they understand the proximate causes (principles) common sense experience has taught them gets to play team out of the 'slump.'

Analogously considered, business professionals do the same thing when they return to their 'Mission Statements' to resolve their problems when they find their organizations confronted by an economic 'slump.'

In both these cases, the professionals involved analogously behaving the way in which, in Book 1, Chapter 1, nns. 2–3 of his *Summa contra gentiles*, Aquinas describes the behavior, 'job,' 'moral responsibility'/'duty' (*officium*, in Latin) wise man. According to him, such a man recognizes that one and the same science as a twofold 'job': (1) to seek to cause some good and truth and (2) fight against and eradicate the contrary opposite of these—evil and falsehood.

Well-known to avid sports fans is that, when a player or team is in a 'slump,' the player, coach, and manager instinctively tend to attempt to solve the problem by having the player or team return to practicing 'the basics.' By 'the basics' they understand the proximate causes (principles) that common sense experience has taught them gets the player or team out of the 'slump.'

In both cases, the professionals involved analogously behaved in the same way in which, in Book 1, Chapter 1, nns.2–3 of his *Summa contra gentiles*, Aquinas describes the behavior, 'job,' 'moral responsibility'/'moral duty' (*officium*) of a wise man. According to him, such a man recognizes that one and the same same science as a two-fold 'job': (1) to seek cause some good and truth and (2) to fight against and eradicate the contrary opposite of these—evil and falsehood.

This is true of all professionals who claim to be practitioners of any art or science. Hence, analogously, it applies to all cultural and civilization leaders. If cultures, civilizations, find themselves in a cultural or civilizational slump, this is chiefly because what their educational institutions inculcate in their students as their purported cultural and civilizational organizational principles (causes) are, in fact, false and bad.

Such cultures and civilizations resemble engineering schools that reduce the science of engineering and causes of bridge-building to principles of language, not to the science of physics. While being able linguistically to communicate ideas and judgments to others by means of intelligible speech is 'a necessary condition' to teach science to students, 'in and of itself, it is an insufficient condition' for so doing.

Evident is that what makes people 'organizational professionals' actually what they are and not oxymoronic, 'organizational fools' is that real, 'organizational professionals are wise and good leaders.'

Such professionals habitually recognize that the twofold activity St. Thomas describes above is a moral duty, ethical responsibility, and an essential part of the professional ethics of their art or science.

More than this, in a way, this moral duty, ethical responsibility, is a proximate cause of what they do as good leaders, prudent men—seekers of truth and human happiness. For this reason, such people are capable of recognizing when an organization they lead is in a slump and how to help that organization get out of a slump. In addition, they want to get their organizations out of a slump because being in one does not make themselves or their customers happy! If they do not get out of slumps, eventually they will go out of business.

The moral virtue of prudence is the proximate cause of all virtue and part of the essential means for getting out of all slumps. All science is a psychological habit of virtuous, prudent, leadership. For this reason, an 'imprudent scientist' is an oxymoron—a foolish, stupid, untruthful, evil, scientific leader.

All sciences are psychological habits of understanding truth and goodness that chiefly (first and foremost) exist as first principles, causes, in the psychological dispositions and activities of scientists. When St. Thomas says that the job of a philosopher, or scientist, is to study causes of truth and goodness, strictly speaking, he means that philosophers, scientists, chiefly study the causes of the actions of substances considered as organizational wholes.

For this reason, toward the beginning of his *Commentary on the Metaphysics of Aristotle* (Lesson 3, nns. 54–55), Aquinas starts to engage in the history of the development of the psychological habit of philosophizing among the Ancient Greeks and other Mediterranean cultures even prior to them. He does so by first describing how Aristotle explains the chief psychological aim that causes everyone to seek to become a philosopher: a twofold desire that develops within us as individuals and community members to acquire a knowledge of causes and their effects.

Simply put as best I can, Aquinas states that: (1) A desire begins within individuals as a community of people to escape from the evil and unhappiness they recognize ignorance of causes has tended to create in them. As a result, they gradually start collectively 'wondering' about causes and their effects on different substances (organizational wholes). (2) By slow progress in collectively escaping from ignorance and its damaging effects by means of this method, by habitually practicing this act of wondering 'as a growing team activity,' this organizational whole of 'budding social scientists' slowly acquires the contrary opposite understanding of them as principles of activity of substances.

St. Thomas's description of Aristotle's report about the way Ancient Mediterranean communities started to do this is as follows:

(1) They first wondered about causes of easier, less highly intellectual, uncomplicated activities of substances (organizational wholes) close at hand to them with which they were very familiar and whose actions were more immediately evident to their senses as 'uncomplicated, movements.' Understanding such activities in this way, and their qualities, required little imagination and not much memory or experience on their part.

(2) Making progress using this procedure, "slow by slow"—as my friend John N. Deely was fond of saying—they started to wonder

about more difficult activities and qualities of substances (organizational wholes) less readily close at hand to them.

These activities involved 'apparent motions' and 'apparent qualities' (such as apparent shapes and sizes) of heavenly bodies. These bodies, movements, and qualities were far distances away from them physically and more remote from immediate, clear, sense observation by them. As a result, understanding this behavior required use of more complicated, internal sensory and psychological acts of imagination, memory, and rational analysis than did understanding movements and qualities of bodies precisely observable to them close by.

As examples of such phenomena about which they wondered, Aquinas lists the following: Lunar eclipses and apparent changes in the shape and size of the Moon as it stands (rests) in different relations to the Sun; Solar eclipses and apparent changes in the shape and size of the Sun as it appears to move; the apparent arrangement and movement, proximity and distance, of the Stars; and the origin of the entire Universe—which some Ancient investigators had attributed to Chance, an Intelligence, and even Love.

In my next Installment, I will continue meditating on Aristotle's and Aquinas's report of the historical development of philosophy, science, among Ancient Western communities as a cultural and social science habit and virtue of wondering about causes of organizational movements and activities.

# Meditation Installment 38

*Groundbreaking Meditation on St. Thomas Aquinas's Report of Aristotle's Depiction of the Origin of the World-Historical Concept of Philosophy, Science!*

When, in Lesson 1 of his *Commentary on the Metaphysics of Aristotle* (especially n.11) St. Thomas Aquinas begins his report of how Aristotle had begun talking about the history of the origin of the concept of philosophy, science, among the Ancient Greeks and other Mediterranean cultures prior to them, he had described this as an individual and community team enterprise: a 'prudent,' organizational act of an organizational whole. The people involved in starting this organization shared a common, prudent, chief aim: to escape from the damaging effects they had commonly recognized brute-animal ignorance causes.

They could not have proceeded in this way had they not shared a common concept and understanding of human beings as a unique species of animal: 'a rational animal.' In addition, to talk somewhat like a student of Georg Hegel (b.1770; d.1831), they had thought of themselves as conceiving of philosophy, science, as 'a world-historical concept.'

'Strictly speaking,' they had not conceived of themselves as: (1) an organizational community engaged in some sort of cultural revolution; (2) Europeans; or (3) Westerners. They could not have done so because, 'strictly speaking,' none of these concepts had precisely existed during their time.

When philosophy had first started to arise among ancient Greeks colonists in Asia-Minor (near modern-day Turkey, in Miletus and Ionia) around the 7th and 6th centuries, B.C., the Ancient Greeks had conceived of the world as they knew it to consist in lands surrounding the Aegean Sea. This became the later-known 'Mediterranean' ('Middle Land') geographical region: 'the Middle of the Roman Empire' as the Romans later conceived of it.

To the peoples living in the lands surrounding the Aegean Sea during the time of the start of Ancient Greek philosophy, the concept of 'the World' consisted of: (1) 'lands to the East' (Asia); (2) 'lands to the South' (Libya); and (3) 'lands to the West and North' (the geographical region that later became called 'Europe').

Etymologically, the word 'Europe' is derived from *Europa*—the name of a Phoenician (modern Lebanon) princess who was the mother of King Minos of Crete, whom the god Zeus had abducted as a wife. In addition, the Ancient Greeks had referred to 'Euros' as their northernmost province of Thrace and to the river that flowed through it. Before the term 'Europe' became used to refer to a continent (around the ninth century, A.D.) it was often used to refer to Thrace.

During the ninth-century Carolingian Renaissance, the term 'Europe' started to designate 'the area of cultural and political influence and continent' controlled in the 'Western Roman Empire' by the Roman Catholic Church (the modern West) as distinct from 'the areas of political and cultural influence and geographical regions of the 'Eastern Roman Empire,' mainly influenced by Eastern Orthodox Catholic Churches and Islam.

I have taken the time in this installment to point out the above facts about the increasingly precise historical development in understanding ideas like 'Europe,' 'the West,' and 'the World' to drive home more deeply into the consciousness of my readers the fact that when we first start to conceive of any new subject, or substance, and its activities, we always do so 'conflatedly'—using all our psychological knowing and emotional faculties united in numerically one act of sense-understanding.

We first sense a new subject, or substance, and all qualities 'generically' with our intellect and intellectualize them with all our internal and external sense faculties before we sense and intellectualize about them specifically and individually. A child first senses 'something' moving toward him or her before conceiving and sensing this being as 'Mommy' or 'Daddy.'

Analogously considered, the way in which the Ancients living around the Aegean Sea first conceived of themselves as 'community wonderers' mirrors the way they first conceived of philosophy, science, as an act of wondering practiced by a world-wide community—not as an act of Westerners, or Europeans, or any regional culture.

They first wondered about themselves as 'wonderers' in general, using easier, uncomplicated psychological acts of imagination, memory, and vivid sense experience—Myth, rhapsodies about the gods sung by wandering, inspired, Rock-star, sons of gods: Great Mythological Poets like Homer and Hesiod, and other 'rappers,' like Orpheus and Musaios, who had preceded them.

In my next Installment, I will meditate about Aristotle's and Aquinas's report of the pre-philosophical, pre-scientific, habit and activity of wondering about causes of organizational behavior that was first started by Mythological Poets centuries before the first Ancient Greek philosophers had come upon the scene.

# Meditation Installment 39

*Aquinas's Meditation about Philosophers, Like Ancient Poets, Being 'Myth-lovers' and 'Pursuers of Wisdom for Its Own Sake'*

After discussing the way Aristotle had depicted the psychological evolution of the Ancient Greeks physicists who had first wondered about the causes of motion and action on Earth and in the heavens, St. Thomas starts to comment about Aristotle's observation that, as someone who wonders, 'in a way' (that is, 'analogously'), a philosopher resembles Ancient theological poets in being a *Philomuthos*. (*Commentary on the Metaphysics of Aristotle*, Lesson 3, nns. 55–68; see Aristotle, *Metaphysics*, 982b11-983a23). Most remarkable to me about Aristotle's depiction of philosophers in this way is how radically different and positive it is about them in contrast to the highly negative opinion that Socrates and Aristotle's beloved teacher, Plato, had held of them.

For example, recall that, along with corrupt 'sophists,' among the chief accusers of Socrates in Plato's dialogue the *Apology* were Ancient theological poets, who had claimed to be 'inspired sons of the gods.' In addition, Plato had considered these Ancient poets to be 'essentially liars,' who, among other mendacious acts, had depicted gods to be evil wife- and child-beaters, and cannibals.

For instance, fearing that Zeus would unseat him as King of the gods, the Titan leader Cronos ate all five of Zeus' children (Hades, Hestia, Demeter, Hera, and Poseidon). Previous to this Cronos had deposed and castrated his father Uranos.

Fearing that his own children would depose him, Cronos started to eat all of them. Luckily for him, Cronos' youngest son, Zeus, he was saved from such a dire fate by his mother, Rhea. She gave birth to Zeus in secret and hid him in a cave in Crete. Then, she shrewdly pretended to give Zeus to Cronos by presenting her husband a rock wrapped in swaddling clothes—which Cronos immediately ate.

Zeus, in turn, was 'no mister nice guy.' Among other dastardly deeds, he crippled his wife Hera's son Hephaistos by tossing him off Mount Olympus for trying to protect Hera from Zeus' unwanted advances.

Socrates was so appalled by such 'ungodly' behavior that, in Plato's dialogue the *Euthyphro*, Socrates reacts with incredulity toward Euthyphro when Euthyphro (who claims to have a masterful knowledge of 'piety' and of the most wonderfully pious acts of the gods) holds the Ancient Greeks gods to be exemplars of holiness. No wonder should exist why Plato had entitled this dialogue *Euthyphro*. In Greek, the word 'pious' (*hosion*) means 'holiness.' Euthyphro is 'His Holiness.' More loosely, Euthyphro is 'Mr. Know-it-all,' 'Wisdom personified.'

Socrates' opinion of the depiction of the Ancient Greek gods was so false and disgusting that, in Book 10 of Plato's *Republic*, Plato had banished them from his Ideal City. In addition, in his dialogues, the gods: (1) exist below the Form of the Good; (2) have to look up to it; and (3) do not interfere in human affairs except to protect us from evils. In addition, Plato's conception of a 'form' is a depersonification of a Greek god as a cause existing in matter that causes a material body to move.

Note should also be made that Aristotle continued Plato's removal of the gods (1) from the Earth and (2) as potential subjects of religious veneration and worship. Aristotle's Unmoved Mover and Intelligences that move heavenly bodies do not know we exist and care nothing about us.

Following the natural order of learning—which proceeds from sense knowledge of the easiest and clearest things to know to those that are more difficult and obscure—like Aristotle, Aquinas's attitude toward the Ancient theologizing poets was more kind and positive. As he recognized, these early researchers had little choice but to attempt to get at truth of things 'to the best of their ability.'

Being unable to read or write, they had to pursue their investigation of truth and proximate causes of the behavior of substances chiefly by means of the use of vivid imagination, strong memories, and song. While these first practitioners of mythologically wondering about causes were initially called *Sophoi* ('Wise Men,' in Greek), St. Thomas knew that, later, Pythagoras of Samos (c. 570-495 B.C.) coined the term 'philosophy' chiefly to designate the pursuit of wisdom for the simple love of being wise, and for no practical or productive purpose.

Aquinas reports that Aristotle made the same point about philosophy being a pursuit of wisdom by referring to the fact that the habit of philosophizing only started to be sought after many practical and productive arts had been discovered and 'arts of leisure' ('contemplative,' 'speculative,' or 'liberal' arts) had been discovered. Then, St. Thomas states, 'for the first time,' human beings started to pursue "this kind of prudence" (that is, 'a new species of prudence'—

'speculative, observational, or contemplative, prudence'!): wisdom—prudence (uncommon common sense) sought for its own sake, for itself alone, and not for any other aim.

At this point, because the historical information was largely not available to him, St. Thomas could not mention the important fact that development of the 'arts of leisure,' the 'liberal arts,' had first started in Egypt centuries before the Ancient Greeks had begun to practice the liberal art of geometry ('geometria'/'earth management,' in Greek). As long ago as 3000 B.C., the Egyptians had used geometry for building, agricultural, and sailing purposes.

In his 'Histories,' Herodotus reports that development of geometry as part of an influential school ('place of leisure'/'scola,' in Latin) began when the Pharaoh, King Sestoris, "divided the land of the Nile Delta into large squares of equal size and gave one square to each family." At the time, "the math for determining the surface area did not yet exist, and the tax collectors were not able to calculate the unequal and odd shapes of farmland submitted for tax returns. According to Herodotus, this is how geometry was invented: to help King Sestoris evaluate the tax returns of his farmers" (fourstringfarm.com: 'Filing Taxes in Ancient Egypt,' in *Heritage Farming*, April 15, 2014).

While Herodotus does not mention this fact, a main purpose for education in Ancient Egypt was to create a leisured class of scribes and priests to assist in the function of government. For this reason, many Ancient Egyptian schools were located near government buildings and many of the scribes and priests who worked in them had experience in government. Hence, not only does the West and the world owe to the Ancient, pagan Egyptians thanks for being the historical proximate cause for the beginning of the liberal arts in general. We owe them for starting the first schools of liberal arts and higher education worldwide.

In my next Installment, I plan to continue Aquinas's meditation on philosophy as the pursuit of wisdom for its own sake.

# Meditation Installment 40

*Further Meditation on Aquinas's Teaching That Philosophy is Chiefly 'Pursuit of Wisdom for Its Own Sake'*

In Installment 39, among other topics, I had meditated on St. Thomas Aquinas's commenting about Aristotle's observations: (1) that, as someone who wonders, a philosopher resembles an Ancient theological poet in having the quality of being a 'Myth-lover' (*Philomuthos*, in Greek); and (2) that Pythagoras was the first of the Ancients to designate this science 'philosophy'—instead of 'wisdom' (*sophia*, in Greek) as the other Ancients before him had done— (*Commentary on the Metaphysics of Aristotle*, Lesson 3, nns. 55–57).

In this Installment 40, I will reflect on four additional qualities this science possesses and adds to the behavioral psychology of a true philosopher: (1) causing real human freedom; (2) causing the greatest species of human wealth and greatest of human goods—liberation from all forms of slavery and an elevation of individual human nature to a divine-like state of liberty; (3) adding to the human intellect the most divine and honorable subjects to know and the psychological means to know them—God-like, contemplative understanding; and (4) being the most divine and honorable of all sciences and ways of human understanding (*Commentary on the Metaphysics of Aristotle*, Lesson 3, nns. 58–68).

St. Thomas maintains that 'real freedom' is the first quality the science of philosophy adds to the behavioral psychology of a true philosopher because a person who is really free is a person who does not exist or work for someone else. He or she exists and works for himself or herself. For example, he says, 'slaves' do not exist or work for themselves. They exist for their 'masters' because they work for 'masters' and give to their 'masters' whatever their work produces.

In contrast, the second quality the science of philosophy adds to the behavioral psychology of a true philosopher is 'to enable him or her to exist for himself or herself.' Really free people are 'entrepreneurs.' They work for themselves and receive for themselves whatever profit their work provides.

Free men and women are 'enterprising, self-providers.' Like such people, the science of philosophy (wisdom) works for no other science. Among all human sciences, only philosophy works for itself. Wisdom is free and makes free those who possess it!

Only 'contemplative sciences'—those that pursue knowledge for its own sake, and not for any practical or productive work beyond themselves—are 'better than useful arts' (such as arts of manufacturing). In addition, among these sciences, the science that has as its chief subject of investigation the qualitatively most universal and widely and deeply influential of all causes (the chief cause of the existence and preservation of the entire, finite universe and all causes that exist within this universe) is the highest, best, and most perfect science: First Philosophy, Metaphysics, Wisdom. Only this science exists perfectly and completely for itself!

Given this second quality, St. Thomas maintains that the science of philosophy must give to the behavioral psychology and 'soul' of its possessor its third quality: being, by nature, totally incapable of thinking and behaving like a slave. The true philosopher is psychologically disposed to understand that being a philosopher is really better as a chief aim in life than becoming economically wealthy and every other qualitatively lesser good.

At the same time, the true philosopher is no fool. He or she understands that, in and of itself, the habit of philosophizing 'bakes no cakes and builds no bridges.' While the science of metaphysics might be the qualitatively highest science, and 'properly speaking,' identical with science in its most perfect species, 'properly understood' all true philosophy is a species of situational prudence.

It has its own *officium*/office/moral duty (professional ethics) related to its use. Metaphysical addiction can make a person just as much a slave and a fool as can any other human addiction. To be properly exercised 'freely,' for it to be more than useful, its possessor must know its limits of right use—must use the habit of metaphysics prudently; must understand when, where, and how to use it.

Because the science of philosophy has as its chief subject, aim, final cause, understanding causes and principles of the existence and behavior of everything in this providentially ordered universe, St. Thomas maintains that the chief subject, aim and final cause of philosophy must include understanding God. Having this included as part of its chief subject must make philosophy 'the most divine and honorable science.'

Indeed, Aquinas argues that the science of philosophy is the most honorable science precisely because its subject of study includes the most divine subject of wonder: 'God and matters related to God.' Since philosophers wonder about causes and first principles, they must wonder about God.

Consequently, the science of philosophy must be about God alone or, at a minimum, about God as the qualitatively best, highest, most perfect, universal, and influential of all causes: the chief and providential cause of the existence and preservation of the entire, finite universe, and all the finite causes that exist within it.

While some sciences are more necessary than this science for use in practical and productive life, none is more honorable and excellent than this one considered simply as a science because, more than any other science, it is in no way servile. It is the only human science sought for its own sake and not as tool, or means, to acquire anything beyond its own good.

Having the nature it does, St. Thomas proceeds to demonstrate that, as a habit of investigation initially caused by a desire to understand first principles and causes of everything, the habit of philosophy comes to rest, is perfectly realized, when it arrives at the contrary opposite of the initial cause of its wondering—understanding the first principles and causes of everything.

According to Aquinas, every species of motion exists as the in-between part of a starting point and end point of a contrary opposite relation. Motion is not arbitrary or chaotic. It is always a sequential, providentially orderly, progression from one point (beginning, contrary opposite) to another point (ending, contrary opposite)—like takeoff and landing of an airplane.

Scientific, philosophical, investigation is a species of progressive movement toward understanding—like the in-between flight of the airplane 'from' takeoff 'to' landing. Once the plane lands, the flight is over. Once the chief aim (final cause/chief purpose) of the wonder is realized/understood, the investigation (in-between motion) is over.

According to St. Thomas, the flight of philosophy from an initial habit of wondering about the causes and principles of all things started with Ancient theological poets and pagan priests wondering about less important matters close at hand and easily understandable to them. From these, 'slow by slow,' it gradually progressed to wonder about more hidden causes.

Because they are initially extremely unfamiliar to us, when they first confront us psychologically, we have no memory of such hidden causes. Consequently, we must first perceive them as entirely alien, strange, foreign.

They first appear to us as if they happen, move, mysteriously, by chance. As a result, St. Thomas says that we human beings wonder most of all when things happen in some unexpected way that we cannot anticipate. We initially attribute such happenings to chance, mysteries—events, perhaps, even having no cause whatsoever.

Aquinas adds that we tend to wonder especially about movements and activities that appear to us to have no 'determined, or definite' cause. When the Ancients were first not able to recognize the cause of 'any' action at all, they wondered about all actions as totally alien, as if they were undetermined, chance occurrences. They first wondered in this way even about changes, movements, close at hand that are relatively easy to understand by anyone who has some familiarity (memory, experience) with such behavior.

That is, the most primitive of Ancient wonderers had first wondered about relatively easily understandable physical behavior and movements in the same way as more advanced Ancient astronomers had wondered about the causes of Lunar and Solar eclipses and Ancient geometricians had wondered about whether the diagonal of a square could be commensurate with one of its sides. Once they understood the causes of these phenomena, they ceased to wonder about them. Continuing to do so would have been the act of a fool.

One final point readers of this Installment should note about the brilliance of St. Thomas Aquinas is that, by the time he had completed Lesson 3 of his *Commentary on the Metaphysics of Aristotle* (maybe two dozen pages), he had already laid the foundation rationally to justify the later claim he will make that philosophy as Aristotle had understood it was 'a preamble' to the existence of the qualitatively higher Divine Science of Revealed Theology ('God-talk')—the science in which a providential God talks (reveals knowledge) 'about Himself and matters related to God.' And he had been able to do so precisely because 'every science, division of philosophy, essentially studies some subject and matters related to it!'

# Meditation Installment 41

*On How Aristotle and Aquinas Used Historical Study of the Nature of Causes Progressively to Explain Philosophy's Nature as 'Metaphysical Wonder' about Contrary Opposites*

Long before Aristotle had arrived at his investigation into the nature of unity in Book 10 of his *Metaphysics*, he had concluded that, from its inception among the Ancients, the Myth-lovers and first Greek philosophers had considered the job, or *officium*, of someone wise is 'perfectly' to understand the nature of contrary opposition. This is so true that, in Book 1, Lesson 3, n. 66, of his *Commentary on the Metaphysics of Aristotle*, St. Thomas Aquinas states that all science contains a progressive movement, or 'progression,' in which it naturally seeks to terminate its movement in perfect understanding in which it rests.

Such 'progression' is not identical with temporal progression. Progression in time is always from past to the present and present to the future. As the Western Enlightenment (the true Western philosophical and scientific Dark Age) clearly indicates, progression in time is no guarantee of progress in perfection of philosophical or scientific understanding.

'Strictly speaking,' generically considered, 'progress' toward 'perfect understanding' as a final cause, aim, or goal in philosophy, science, begins in wonder about the causes of the existence, unity, and behavior of everything. And it terminates in putting that wonder to rest by bringing to perfect completion metaphysical understanding of the First Cause and Highest Truth about everything.

The reason progress in philosophy, science, can terminate in perfect understanding as the contrary opposite of the way its wondering starts is twofold: (1) because, 'good, better, and best' are qualitative perfections that belong to species and individuals that exist within a real genus of more than two members; and (2) 'good and better' are qualitative perfections that exist within a real genus of only two members. (See St. Thomas's discussion of division of a real genus by real good and evil in his *Commentary on the Metaphysics of Aristotle*, Book 9, Lesson 10, n.1883 and in Book 10).

According to Aristotle and Aquinas, Ancient Western philosophy, science, had started with some Ancient investigators as parts of communities who had chiefly 'wondered about the causes of everything'—not simply of 'some things.' Because the first of these people had considered everything that existed to be physical—because they could not imagine or conceive of anything being non-physical, immaterial, or spiritual; and did not even have words in their native languages to refer to such beings—they understood all causes to be physical. Hence, they could have no image or concept to use to find the means to form words to use to talk about a philosophical discipline called 'metaphysics.'

Well-known to anyone who has studied the teachings of Aristotle is that he devoted a lot of time talking about four main ways in which people tend to speak about causes as principles—(1) material cause; (2) efficient cause; (3) formal cause; and (4) final cause.

The material cause refers to the physical parts 'of which' some physical whole is com-posed. (2) The efficient cause is a principle 'from which' this physical whole comes to be (the 'action' that unites its parts into a composite whole). (3) The formal cause is the organizational unity to which we refer when we seek to express 'what something is'; and (4) The final cause—qualitative perfection of its 'being what it is' (its form)—is to be perfectly good at being the organizational whole it is. According to Aristotle, the first of the Ancient Greek physicists who had wondered about these causes did so in terms of the well-known, Ancient four physical elements: (1) Earth; (2) Air; (3) Fire; and (4) Water. No universal agreement had existed among Ancient physicists as to which, if any of these, element(s) caused the others.

Nevertheless, they shared the common agreement of the Ancient Greeks that: (1) the physical universe is everlasting, perpetually existing; (2) the nature of all matter is chiefly to move; (3) whatever moves is alive (they were 'vitalists'); (4) what causes something to move is the presence of a god within it; and (5) within a human being this god became reductively referred to as a 'soul.'

In fact, I think that the influence of the presence of the gods within the everlasting, finite universe of the Ancient Greeks was so widespread, deep, and implicitly metaphysical that Plato had eventually arrived at his understanding of a 'form' by conceiving of such a cause negatively as a 'depersonification' of an Ancient Greek god.

Whatever the case regarding the provenance of Plato's concept of a form, if someone were to have asked an Ancient Greek where the entire universe had come from, with bemusement, he or she would likely instinctively have replied: 'From what was here before.' If the inquirer were somewhat pigheaded enough to persist and ask, 'Where did that come from?', the Ancient Greek would likely have replied, 'From what was here before that, of course!'—*ad infinitum*.

Regarding different Ancient Greek physicists who had held one or more of the four elements to be the first cause of everything, Aristotle mentions several to which I do not need to refer. They tend to be well-known. However, Aristotle singles out Thales of Miletus (b. ca. 624–620 B.C.; d. 548–545 B.C.; often referred to today as the 'Father of Philosophy' or 'Father of Western Philosophy') to be the 'originator' of the 'speculative' (observational) philosophy of physics.

Aristotle did so because he had maintained that Thales had been the only one among the seven Ancient 'Wise Men' (*Sophoi*, in Greek) who: (1) historically came after the theological poets (self-proclaimed 'inspired sons of the gods'—whose inspiration was the only cause for anyone being a member of the *Sophoi*); (2) had investigated the nature of physical things as such—simply to understand this nature; and (3) had committed his arguments to writing. The other Ancient sages had focused their attention on the practical study of moral matters, ethics.

While he does not mention so explicitly, another reason Aristotle had to single out Thales for this honorific title was because, since the ancients had reduced everything to matter, they had conflated physics and metaphysics. Thales had done the same thing; and, in order clearly to identify himself as a follower of this theological tradition, beyond stating that water is the cause of everything, Thales was famous for having added, "And all things are full of gods." Hence, as Aristotle recognized, in a way, Thales was the only one of the Ancient *Sophoi* who, following in the footsteps of the theological poets before them, had practiced philosophy chiefly as a metaphysician.

In so doing, Thales helped move the philosophical quest of the psychological habit of metaphysical wondering to come to rest in perfect metaphysical understanding of the whole truth about everything.

www.ingramcontent.com/pod-product-compliance
Lightning Source LLC
LaVergne TN
LVHW051829080426
835512LV00018B/2788